PRIMARY
SCIENCE SAMPLER

WRITTEN BY SANDRA MARKLE
ILLUSTRATED BY BEV ARMSTRONG

THE LEARNING WORKS

P.O. BOX 6187 SANTA BARBARA, CALIF. 93111

TABLE OF CONTENTS

The Primary Science Sampler is designed to provide the teacher with a programmed approach to a challenging hands-on experience in science.

There are six units dealing with heat and cold, animals, human senses, forces, plants, and kitchen chemistry. Each unit contains:

1. Brief background information for the teacher

2. A list of words that may be unfamiliar to the students

3. A specific set of learning objectives

4. Predictions to provide students with an opportunity to brainstorm, estimate results, and consider possibilities before they experiment

5. Display and bulletin board ideas

6. Extra Spark Starters to light the fire of curiosity

7. A list of materials needed for the entire set of experiments in each unit

8. Additional sources: books and audio-visual materials

9. The answers to questions and puzzles

10. An evaluation section to indicate if students have mastered the learning objectives

11. Extending Learning suggestions for more creative and challenging ways to continue the unit and incorporate language arts, math, social studies, and art

The investigations are coded *I* for those that can be completed by students without assistance, *TD* for experiments that may need teacher direction, and *A* for those that are more challenging. Depending upon the number and the maturity of the students, teachers may have to provide direction and assistance in many of the experiments, and may have to read the directions out loud.

The Primary Science Sampler's goal is to equip you, the teacher, with as many time-saving tools as possible so that you can enjoy sharing the challenges of these units with your students.

HOT AND COLD

BACKGROUND

Everything is made up of tiny particles called *atoms* and groups of atoms called *molecules.* The arrangement of these atoms and the spaces between them determines the kind of matter which is formed.

In a *solid*, the atoms or molecules are packed tightly together. In a *liquid*, the particles are more widely spaced. In a *gas*, the particles are far apart.

The faster atoms and molecules move, the more they bump into each other and spread apart. Ice is an example of a solid. If ice is heated, the molecules begin to move faster until the ice changes to water. If more heat is added, the water molecules speed up, the spaces widen, and water vapor — a gas — forms.

Heat can be caused by *friction.* Whenever objects rub together, this rubbing action — *friction* — causes the molecules or atoms to speed up.

Chemical reactions also can speed up particles and create heat. A chemical reaction is the combination of two or more substances, which causes a change or creates a completely new substance.

Heat is measured in *degrees* and a thermometer tells us how many degrees of heat something has.

The first known work to measure heat was done by Galileo Galilei in 1593. His thermoscope was a narrow glass tube filled with liquid. It was able to show changes in temperature without accurately measuring them. Because it was an open tube, air molecules pressed on the liquid and prevented it from expanding as completely as it would in a vacuum (a complete absence of atoms and molecules).

Gabriel Daniel Fahrenheit invented the first accurate thermometer in 1714. He used a sealed glass tube into which he had inserted mercury and from which he had withdrawn all the air. Fahrenheit created a scale for measuring temperature based on the lowest temperature possible for a mixture of salt and water and at the opposite extreme the blood temperature of humans.

In 1742, Anders Celsius developed the Celsius scale of measurement. It was developed particularly to measure the high melting temperatures of metals.

The boiling point of water is 212° F. and 100° C. The freezing temperature of water is 32° F. and 0° C.

Cold is the absence of heat. In the investigations in this unit, students explore the fact that cold water molecules move more slowly than warm water molecules. They discover that water expands as it freezes and that salt water freezes at a lower temperature than fresh water. It is also interesting that the salt separates and rises to the top as the water freezes.

Which freezes faster: hot water or cold water? Surprise — hot water does. The faster molecular movement of the hot water exchanges the heat more quickly with the air.

Before refrigeration, blocks of ice were stacked in layers of sawdust. They often lasted through the spring and into the summer.

Students are challenged in this unit to find a way to keep ice from melting. To motivate their creativity, you could make the following suggestions: (1) stack several cubes together; (2) put the ice in a cup and cover it to prevent air movement over the cube; (3) wrap the ice in layers of paper to insulate the ice.

WORD BOX:

degrees	temperature	friction
thermometer	freeze	chemical reaction
Celsius	Fahrenheit	

LEARNING OBJECTIVES:

1. Students will be able to read a thermometer.

2. Students will understand how friction and chemical reactions cause heat.

3. Students will be able to determine what happens to the salt as salt water freezes.

4. Students will understand what affects the freezing of water and how water changes as it freezes.

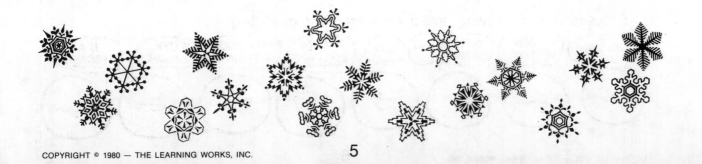

PREDICTIONS:

1. Do you think that rubbing something can make it warm?

2. Do you think that adding rubbing alcohol to water will make the water warmer?

3. Which do you think will move faster, the molecules in warm water or in cool water?

4. Do you think that water will take up more or less space as it freezes?

5. Which do you think will freeze faster, fresh or salt water?

DISPLAY AND BULLETIN BOARD IDEAS:

1. Put a giant posterboard thermometer on one wall. Cover the center with flannel and have sections of red flannel to fit on this part of the thermometer.

   Let students take turns reading the temperature on an outside thermometer and then make the giant thermometer match this reading. You may also want to include a sign that displays the expected daily high and low temperature in Fahrenheit and Celsius readings.

2. Divide a bulletin board into two parts. Label one section HOT and the other COLD. Put up pictures that illustrate things and places that are warm, hot, cool, or cold. Encourage your students to bring in other examples. Include word cards that illustrate HOT or COLD such as *shiver* and *burn*.

EXTRA SPARK STARTER:

1. Play "Hot or Cold."

   Send one student out of the room. Quickly decide on a mystery object. The student returns and moves around the room. The class calls out clues — "You are getting colder" or "You are very cold" if the student moves away from the mystery object. "You are getting warmer" or "You are hot" would indicate that the student is getting close to the mystery object.

   To keep things moving, set a time limit for guessing.

2. Role play molecular movement:

   1. Move like cold molecules and heat up slowly.

   2. Move like hot molecules cooling off quickly on a signal.

   3. Be ice cubes. Heat is added. Melt and change to water, and then change to water vapor.

   4. Be water vapor. Freeze suddenly and become snow flakes.

3. Make paper ice cubes, large water drops, and snowflakes to hang from the ceiling, to put on a bulletin board, or to tape to the windows for decoration.

MATERIALS NEEDED:

Bowl
*Fahrenheit and Celsius thermometers (there should be enough for at least 1 to every 2 students)
Tape

Measuring cups
Crayons
Freezer
Clock
Tablespoon
Sink
Ice cubes
Pencil

Rubbing alcohol
Metal or plastic ice cube tray with dividers
Paper or plastic cups
Salt
Black and white construction paper
Metric ruler

*One of the least expensive and fastest ways to obtain these is to purchase small indoor-outdoor thermometers at a hardware or discount store. These are usually in a plastic case, but they can easily be removed from their case. These are also more likely to be alcohol thermometers, which are safer than mercury thermometers, should one accidentally break.

ADDITIONAL SOURCES: BOOKS

Adler, Irving. Heat and Its Uses. John Day, 1973.

Fervolo, Rocco V. Heat. Gerrard, 1964.

Liss, Howard. Heat. Coward, 1965.

Pine, Tillie S., and Joseph Levine. Heat All Around. McGraw, 1963.

Scott, John M. Heat and Fire. Parents Press, 1973.

ADDITIONAL SOURCES: FILMSTRIPS

Matter and Energy. Primary and intermediate level. Set of 6 filmstrips and sound. SVE—Society For Visual Education, Inc.

ANSWERS:

Ask students to answer the thought questions in complete sentences.

p. 10: Your hands now feel warmer. (true)

The water will feel warmer as alcohol is added. The amount needed to cause this chemical reaction will vary depending on the temperature of the water.

p. 11: The answers will vary with the thermometers.

p. 12: The thermometer shown is a Celsius thermometer.
Each line shows two degrees.
The temperature at arrow A is 24° C.
The temperature at arrow B is 30° C.
The temperature at arrow C is 66° C.
There are six degrees difference between A and B.
Coloring in the thermometer will vary.

p. 13: Answers will vary.

p. 15: The answers may vary slightly depending on the freezer and how quickly the thermometer is read after it is removed from the freezer. In general, water freezes at 0° C. and 32° F. The initial freezing temperature will be the same as the temperature when the freezing is complete.

5. Ice formed first on the top and edge of the water.

p. 16: The glass with ice bulging above the top should be circled in the Challenge Picture.
The water in the cups expanded beyond the top.
Three cups were used to be sure that the results were not accidental. If the same thing happened three times, it must usually happen.

p. 17: 1. The liquid on top in the salt cup tastes salty.
2. The ice in the salt cup tastes fresh.
3. The salt water took longer to freeze than the fresh water.
The salt separated from the water as the water froze.

p. 19: Ideas will vary.

p. 20: Answers will vary. Check for accurate measurements and thoughtful answers.

p. 21: 1. After five minutes, the bigger puddle of water was on the black paper.
2. The cube that melted away first was on the black paper.
3. On a hot day, it would be more comfortable to wear a white shirt or blouse.

EVALUATION:

Answer each question carefully. Print the answer on the blank to the right of each question.

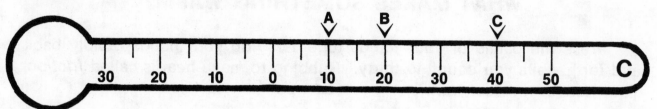

1. What temperature is at arrow A?   (10° C.)
2. What temperature is at arrow B?   (20° C.)
3. What temperature is at arrow C?   (40° C.)
4. How many degrees does each line represent?   (5° C.)
5. How many degrees are between A and C?   (30° C.)

Find the word or words that correctly complete each statement. Put the letter of the answer on the blank.

A. Faster   C. Friction   E. More
B. More slowly   D. Thermometer   F. Less

1. A _____(D)_____ measures temperature.
2. Salt water freezes _____(B)_____ than fresh water.
3. Hot water molecules move _____(A)_____ than cold water molecules.
4. _____(C)_____ is a rubbing together of objects that makes heat.
5. Water takes up _____(E)_____ space when it freezes.

EXTENDED LEARNING:

1. Make ice cream.
2. Investigate how much heat objects can hold.
3. Investigate which objects hold heat longer.
4. Make candles.
5. Which freezes faster: hot or cold water?
6. Which color absorbs more heat: black or white?
7. How does salt affect ice?
8. Write a story about a young pioneer boy alone in the woods. It is getting dark and he needs to start a fire. How can he do it without matches?

WHAT MAKES SOMETHING WARM?

Press the palms of your hands together. Rub your hands rapidly back and forth while you count to thirty. Rubbing to make heat is called *friction*. Your hands now feel warmer. ☐ true ☐ false

Sometimes a *chemical reaction* makes heat. In a chemical reaction, two or more things join to make something new. Try this chemical reaction.

You will need a bowl, rubbing alcohol, and two measuring cups (1 cup and ¼ cup).

Directions:

1. Pour one cup of cool water into the bowl and touch the water with your finger.

2. Add one-fourth cup of rubbing alcohol and touch the water again.

3. The water feels ☐ warmer ☐ the same

4. If the water is not warmer, add more alcohol one-fourth cup at a time. Keep testing with your finger.

5. How many one-fourth cups of alcohol did it take to cause a chemical reaction that warmed the water? _____

Name _____

HOW DO WE MEASURE HEAT?

Heat is measured in degrees. A *thermometer* tells how many degrees of heat something has.

Get a thermometer. Look at it closely. There are two kinds of thermometers: Fahrenheit and Celsius. Look for an *F* or a *C* on your thermometer. Which kind do you have? _____

The symbol for degrees is °. Always put this symbol after a temperature. Then put an *F* for Fahrenheit or a *C* for Celsius to show which type of thermometer you used. (Example: 25° F)

How many degrees does each line on your thermometer show? _____

What is the highest temperature reading on your thermometer? _____

What is the lowest temperature reading on your thermometer? _____

Look carefully. If the numbers go down to zero and then start over again, the lowest temperature on your thermometer is written in minus degrees, such as —10° C.

32° F AND 0° C = FREEZING

212° F AND 100° C = BOILING

WHAT TEMPERATURE IS IT?

Look at the picture of the thermometer.

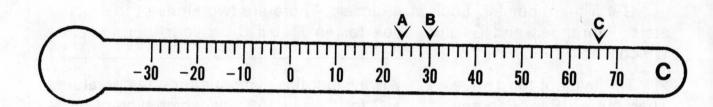

Is this a Fahrenheit or a Celsius thermometer?   _____

How many degrees does each line show?   _____

What temperature is shown at arrow A?   _____

What temperature is shown at arrow B?   _____

What temperature is shown at arrow C?   _____

How many degrees difference is there between
temperature A and B?   _____

Check the weather forecast. Write the date on the line. Color in the thermometer to show the high temperature predicted for the day.

_____
Date

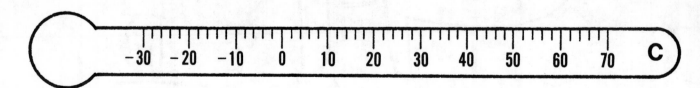

Name _____

HOW HOT IS IT?

When you take the temperature of something, follow these rules:

1. If possible, read the thermometer without touching it with your hands. Your hands add heat. Lay the thermometer on the object or against the side of a container.

2. Between each test, carefully shake the thermometer. This lowers the colored liquid back to its beginning point.

Take the temperature of each item on the list. Then color in the thermometer at the bottom of the page to show the temperature.

A. The inside air: place the thermometer in a room away from heaters and sunny windows. Check after five minutes.

B. The outside air: place the thermometer in the shade outside the building. Check after five minutes.

C. Your body: hold the thermometer in your hand for two minutes.

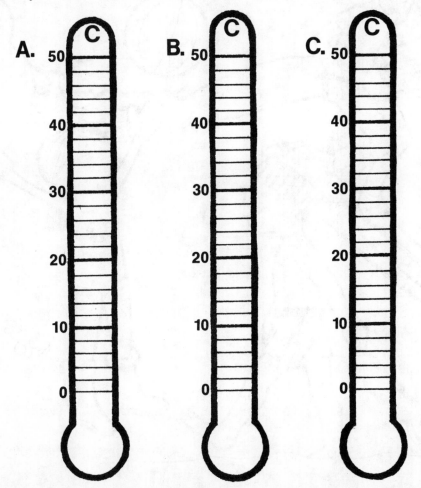

13

Name _____

A DAY AT THE BEACH

Circle each thing that does not belong in this picture.

Name _____

AT WHAT TEMPERATURE DOES WATER FREEZE?

You will need: an ice cube tray (metal or plastic with dividers), a thermometer, a freezer and a clock.

Directions:

1. Put water into the tray so that it is almost full.

2. Put the tray in the freezer and lay the thermometer across the dividers.

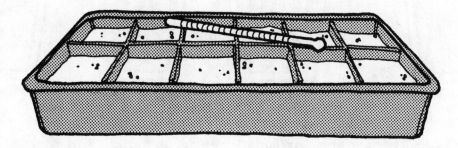

3. Check every thirty minutes. Do not touch the thermometer until ice starts to form in the tray. Then pick it up carefully by the end away from the bulb. Your body heat will quickly change the temperature.

4. At what temperature did the ice start to form? _____

5. Take the tray out and look at it. Ice formed first

    ☐ on the top and edge of the water   ☐ in the middle of the water.

6. Put the tray and thermometer back into the freezer. Continue to check until the cubes are solid.

7. What was the temperature when the water was completely frozen? _____

WHAT HAPPENS TO WATER WHEN IT FREEZES?

Challenge Picture

Circle the picture that you think shows what the glass of water on the left will look like after the water freezes.

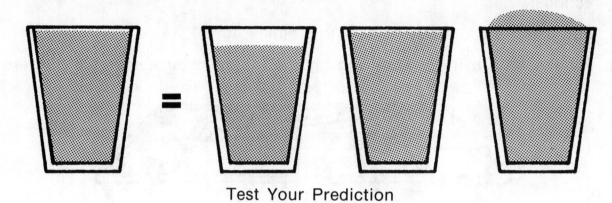

Test Your Prediction

You will need: Three paper or plastic cups, a pencil and a freezer.

Directions:

1. Number the cups: 1, 2, and 3.

2. Fill all three cups to the top with water.

3. Put the cups in the freezer and let them sit until the water is completely frozen.

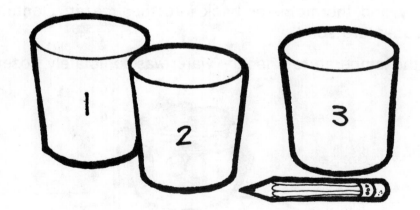

The water in the cups

☐ shrank.   ☐ stayed at the same level.   ☐ expanded beyond the top.

Why do you think you used three cups instead of just one? _____

_____

WHAT HAPPENS TO SALT WATER WHEN IT FREEZES?

You will need: two paper or plastic cups, a pencil, a tablespoon, salt, a freezer, a clock and a sink.

Directions:

1. Label one cup *salt* and the other cup *fresh.*

2. Put one tablespoon of salt into the salt cup.

3. Fill both cups half full of water. Stir the salt water until the salt dissolves.

4. Put both cups in the freezer. Check every thirty minutes until the water is frozen.

Questions:

1. If there is any liquid on top of the ice in the salt cup, dip your finger into it and taste it. Does it taste fresh or salty? _____

2. Pour any liquid on top of the ice in the salt cup into the sink. Rinse the cube. Taste the ice. Does it taste fresh or salty? _____

3. Tell how the salt water froze differently from the fresh water.

_____

_____

FUN PAGE

How many hot and cold words can you find hidden in this glass?
As you find the words, draw lines around them.
Use the Clue Box to help you.

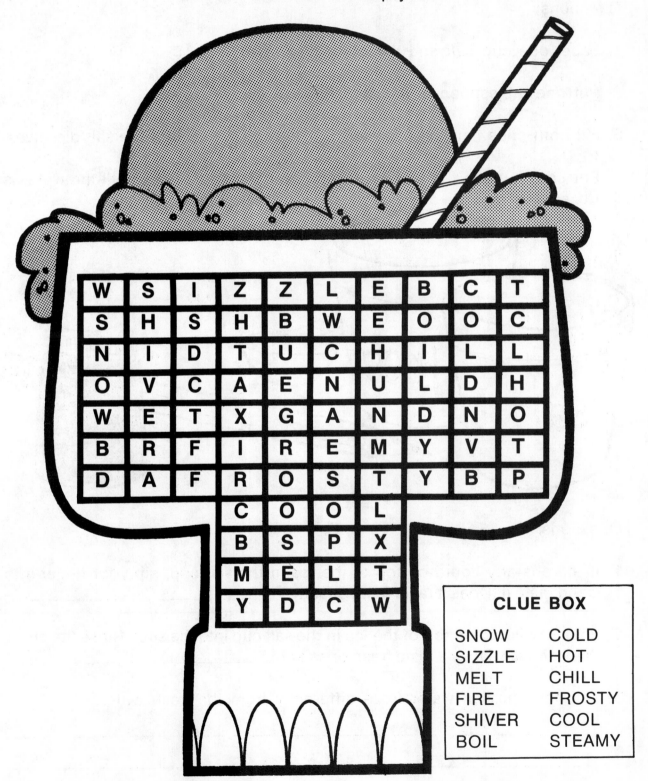

W	S	I	Z	Z	L	E	B	C	T
S	H	S	H	B	W	E	O	O	C
N	I	D	T	U	C	H	I	L	L
O	V	C	A	E	N	U	L	D	H
W	E	T	X	G	A	N	D	N	O
B	R	F	I	R	E	M	Y	V	T
D	A	F	R	O	S	T	Y	B	P
		C	O	O	L				
		B	S	P	X				
		M	E	L	T				
		Y	D	C	W				

CLUE BOX

SNOW	COLD
SIZZLE	HOT
MELT	CHILL
FIRE	FROSTY
SHIVER	COOL
BOIL	STEAMY

Name _____

HOLD ONTO THAT ICE!

Before there were refrigerators, there were iceboxes. An icebox was cooled by a big block of ice. When the ice melted, a new block was put into the icebox. There were no freezers. Where did the ice come from?

In the winter, big blocks of ice were chopped out of frozen lakes and ponds. Sometimes a whole town would get together to chop blocks of ice. The ice was coated with layers of sawdust and stacked like building blocks inside a barn.

Everyone helped. The people worked all day chopping the ice, moving it to the barn, and packing it away.

They would share the ice as long as it lasted. It is hard to believe, but the blocks of ice lasted until the middle of the hot summer.

Make a list of five different ways that you might keep an ice cube from melting.

1. _____

2. _____

3. _____

4. _____

5. _____

Name _____

HOLD ONTO THAT ICE — continued

Let's test your ideas. Get five ice cubes — one cube for each of your ideas.

Use a metric ruler to measure how many centimeters long each cube is. Write this information on the chart.

Try each of your ideas. Measure the cubes again after thirty minutes. Write this information on the chart.

Measure the cubes again after one hour and write this information on the chart.

Which cube did the best? _____

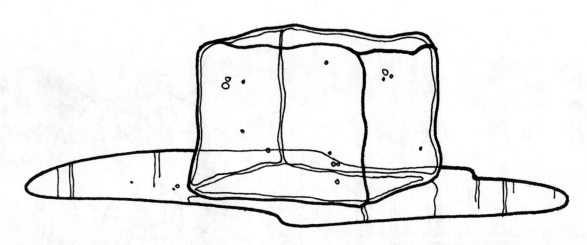

WAYS TO STOP MELTING	CUBES	BEGINNING MEASUREMENT	AFTER THIRTY MINUTES	AFTER ONE HOUR

WHICH WILL SOAK UP HEAT FASTER?

You will need: a piece of white construction paper, a piece of black construction paper, tape, two ice cubes (must be the same size), a pencil and a clock.

Directions:

1. Put the white and black pieces of paper side by side in a sunny spot. This can be outside or by a window. Tape the corners of the paper down.

2. Put an ice cube on the center of each piece of paper.

3. Draw around the cube with a pencil.

4. Check the cubes every five minutes.

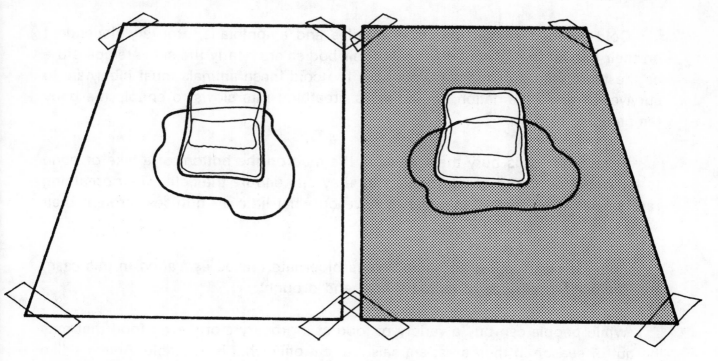

Questions:

1. After five minutes, the bigger puddle of water was

   ☐ on the white paper.   ☐ on the black paper.

2. The cube that melted away first was

   ☐ on the white paper.   ☐ on the black paper.

3. On a hot day, it would be more comfortable to wear

   ☐ a white shirt or blouse.   ☐ a black shirt or blouse.

FUZZ, FEATHERS, AND FINS

BACKGROUND

People can put on different kinds of clothing. They can heat or cool their houses. Animals, however, must have a home that provides all of their needs: the right kind of food, the right amount of water, the right temperature, and protection from enemies. A home that provides all of these things is called a *habitat.*

The main habitats are the forest, the jungle, the desert, the freshwater environments, and the ocean.

Animal life may be warm-blooded or cold-blooded. Warm-blooded animals use their food not only for growth and movement but also to produce body heat. Warm-blooded animals are able to withstand fairly major changes in temperature. Mammals are warm-blooded.

Cold-blooded animals, such as reptiles and amphibians, are very dependent on their habitat to provide body heat. Their bodies are nearly the same temperature as the temperature of the air. When it is too cold these animals must hibernate to survive. During hibernation, the animal's breathing rate slows to enable the body temperature to drop.

Frogs and toads bury themselves in the mud on the bottom of a lake or pond to hibernate during the winter. This way they can endure the cold. Their breathing rate slows so much that they can survive on what little air diffuses through their skin.

Some desert reptiles and amphibians hibernate (called *estivation* in this case) to escape from periods of extreme heat and drought.

While people can buy a variety of food at a grocery store, even food that may be out of season in their area, animals can eat only what is available. Animals, like people, are part of a food chain.

All food chains start with green plants. Only green plants can make their own food. Some animals are very picky eaters. Koala bears eat mainly eucalyptus leaves. Monarch butterfly caterpillars eat only milkweed leaves.

People have killed more animals and endangered their very existence by destroying their habitats and by breaking their food chains than by shooting them.

For example, the southern bald eagle builds a huge nest. Year after year a mating pair returns to the same nest (eagles have only one mate during their lifetime). If that tree is cut down, the eagles will not build a new nest and will never lay eggs again.

WORD BOX:

habitat	food chain	track
specialized	burrow	chlorophyll

LEARNING OBJECTIVES:

1. Students will be able to state the main animal habitats and the general kinds of animals that live in them.

2. Students will understand that all food chains start with green plants.

3. Students will be able to arrange animals in realistic food chains.

4. Students will be aware of some of the interesting variety in animals.

PREDICTIONS:

1. Do you think a bear could live in the desert? Why or why not?

2. Could a shark live in a forest? Why or why not?

3. Cut out pictures of birds and animals. Tape a paper flap over the picture so that just the beak shows on the birds and just the feet on the animals. Ask what kind of food you think each bird eats. Do the same with animal feet. Ask what animal they think the feet belong to.

DISPLAY AND BULLETIN BOARD IDEAS:

1. Divide a bulletin board or display area into five parts — one for each of the main habitats. Label each area and decorate it to look like a desert, jungle, forest, fresh-water environment, or ocean.

   As your students investigate this unit, encourage them to find (or make) pictures of animals that live in each habitat. Add these pictures to the habitat along with a printed card that names the animal.

   Later you may want to ask students to arrange the animals in each habitat into food chains.

2. There are nonfiction and fiction books about animals on a variety of reading levels. Arrange a display of animal books.

3. Mystery animal: Put up clues about a common or well-known animal. Can your students guess which animal it is? You may want to offer a prize or a reward.

EXTRA SPARK STARTER:

1. Have students cut colored pictures of animals, birds, and fish from magazines or draw and color pictures of their own. Then cut the pictures apart and create fanciful new animals with feet from one animal, a head from another, and so forth.

   Older students could write stories about their creatures.

2. Visit a zoo and/or a farm and tape record a variety of animal sounds. Some sound filmstrips include animal sounds. Play the sounds and challenge your students to identify the animals from the sounds they make.

MATERIALS NEEDED:

Scissors	Suet	Bread crumbs
Crayons	Saucepan	Popped corn
Glue	Hot plate	Sunflower seeds
*Sponge dice	Spoon	Sand
Pencil	Green styrofoam egg	Garbage bag ties (8 per
Refrigerator	cartons (2 per	student)
White construction	student)	Tape
paper	Marking pens	

*To make sponge dice, cut cubes of foam rubber. Number each side of the cube with a permanent marking pen. These dice work just as well as regular dice and they are quiet.

ADDITIONAL SOURCES: BOOKS

Podendorf, Illa. Animals and More Animals. Childrens Press, 1970.

Putnam's has published a large number of Biography of A . . . books about animals. They are by different authors and illustrators, and they are all excellent.

ADDITIONAL SOURCES: FILMSTRIPS

How Animals Live and Grow. Primary level. Set of 6 filmstrips and sound. Encyclopedia Britannica Educational Corporation.

The Life of Animals. Grades K-4. Set of 5 filmstrips and sound. National Geographic Society.

ANSWERS:

Ask students to answer thought questions in complete sentences.

p. 27: Animals to be pasted on the habitats:

Ocean — shark

Desert — roadrunner

Freshwater pond — bullfrog

Forest — gray squirrel

Jungle — monkey

p. 28: Draw a line from:

the squirrel to the leafy, mound-shaped nest

the owl to the hole in the tree

the brown bear to the cave

the mouse to the burrow

the spider to the web

the wasp to the paper nest

the robin needs a nest on a tree branch

p. 30:

2	5	1	4	3
Shrimp	Tiger Shark	Algae	Tuna	Cod

Animals in a food chain will vary. A green plant should be first. Check for logical progression: animals should be increasingly bigger, animals should all live in the same habitat.

p. 31: The mystery animal is a chameleon.

p. 32: 1. C   2. F   3. A

4. E   5. D   6. B

p. 34:

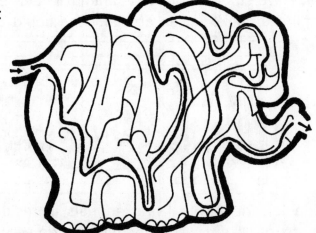

p. 35: Mouse ___1___ Dog ___3___ Cat ___2___

EVALUATION:

Number the food chain in order to show who eats what.

HAWK ___(4)___   GRASS ___(1)___   SNAKE ___(3)___   GRASSHOPPER ___(2)___

Match each animal to the habitat it lives in. Put the letter of the correct answer on the blank.

A. Forest   C. Freshwater Pond   E. Desert
B. Ocean   D. Jungle

1. Brown Bear _____(A)_____

2. Camel _____(E)_____

3. Shark _____(B)_____

4. Monkey _____(D)_____

5. Jellyfish _____(B)_____

6. Screech Owl _____(A)_____

EXTENDED LEARNING:

1. Arrange with student owners (and their parents) to have a small animal pet make a one-day visit. The student owner should be able to tell what kind of habitat his or her pet needs, type of food it eats, and any interesting special facts.

2. Make an alphabet book of animals. Have a construction paper cover and divide the book into sections for each letter of the alphabet. Find pictures of animals whose names start with each letter. Have students print the animal's name under the picture. For letters with no animals, make up an animal. This could be an individual or class project.

3. Visit a zoo or nature center.

4. Visit a farm.

5. Plan and start a class aquarium.

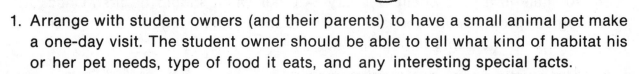

6. Plan and build a class vivarium, a terrarium with living animals in residence. Depending on your habitat, frogs, toads, lizards, and chameleons do very well.

Name _____

WHO LIVES WHERE?

Where an animal lives is its habitat. The habitat is right for that animal if it supplies its needs for food and water. The temperature must not be too hot or too cold. The animal must also be able to get away from its enemies.

Cut out the pictures at the bottom of the page. Paste each animal in the habitat where it would be able to live best.

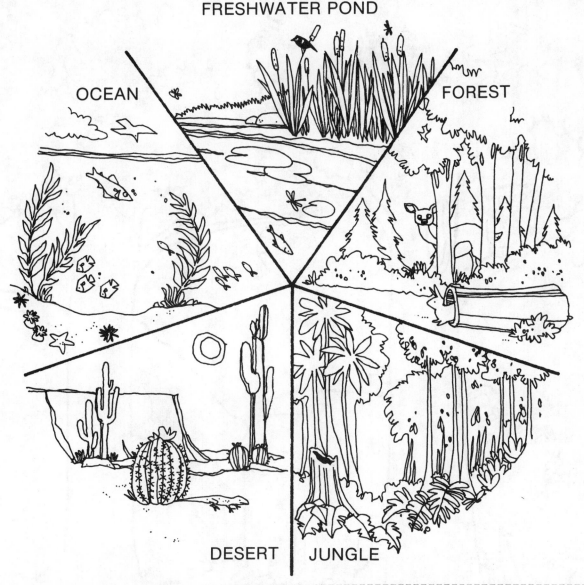

gray squirrel

roadrunner

monkey

bullfrog

shark

Name _____

WHERE IS HOME?

Animals have many different kinds of homes. Draw a line from each animal to its home. Draw a home for the robin.

THE RACE

Field mice have a lot of enemies. Brown mouse and gray mouse are running home. Cut out the two markers. Use the sponge dice to move. Play alone or with a friend. Which mouse can make it home to safety first?

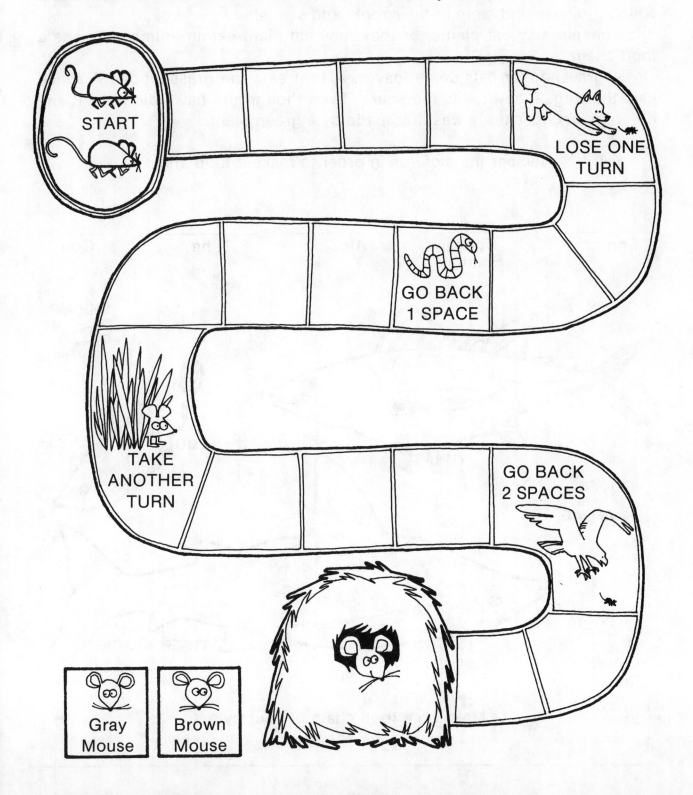

Name _____

WHAT IS A FOOD CHAIN?

All food chains start with green plants. They contain a chemical called chlorophyll. It helps the plants to make their own food. Chlorophyll is put into action by the energy in sunlight. Green plants make sugars and starches, which they use and store in their roots and stems.

Animals may eat plants, or they may eat plant-eating animals. This is a food chain.

A grasshopper eats some leaves. A frog eats the grasshopper. A snake eats the frog. A hawk eats the snake. Even though the hawk did not eat any green plants, its energy was first made by a green plant.

Number the pictures in order to make a food chain.

_____   _____   _____   _____   _____
Shrimp   Tiger   Algae   Tuna   Cod
          Shark

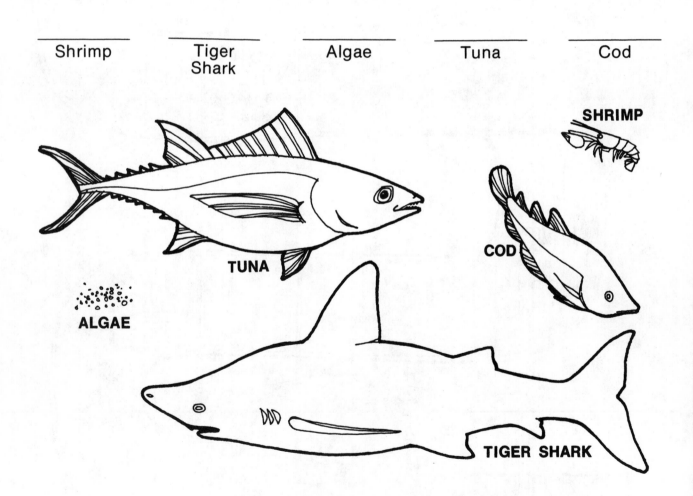

Make up a food chain of your own.

_____   _____   _____   _____   _____

MYSTERY ANIMAL

Connect the dots to see what the mystery animal looks like.
After reading the story, color the picture.

This animal lives in Africa and India. With its curved toes and strong tail, it can grab tightly onto a tree branch.

Its eyes can turn in two different directions at the same time. It catches food by flipping out its long tongue like a spear. It loves to eat insects.

It has a special talent. It can change color. When it is resting, it may be green or brown. When it is afraid, it gets darker with white stripes and black spots. When it is mad, its body is brown, the spots are green, and the stripes are light brown.

What animal is this?

Name _____

THIS IS FOR THE BIRDS

A bird's beak is shaped to fit the kind of food it eats. Cut out each picture at the bottom of page 33. Glue the picture in the space under the description of that kind of beak.

1. The finch has a fat, pointed beak to break open seeds.

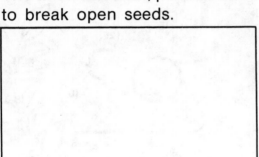

4. A hawk has a sharp, curved beak to tear meat.

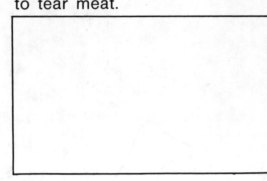

2. The warbler has a thin, pointed beak to pick bugs from leaves.

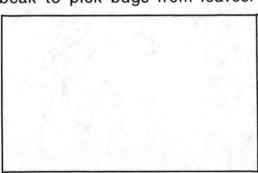

5. The sides of a duck's beak are grooved so the water can run out when it scoops up food.

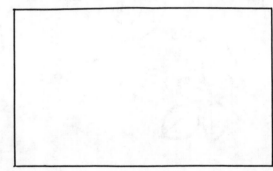

3. A hummingbird's beak is like a long straw. It sips nectar, the sweet juice found in flowers.

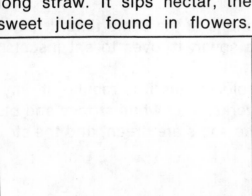

6. A woodpecker has a strong, hard beak so it can drill holes in wood to find insects.

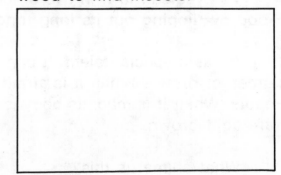

THIS IS FOR THE BIRDS — continued

Here is a recipe that you can make to feed the birds around your house or school.

You will need: one and a half cups of suet (meat fat that you can get at a grocery store), a saucepan and a hot plate, a spoon, one cup of bread crumbs, one cup of popped corn, one cup of sunflower seeds, one teaspoon of sand and a refrigerator.

Directions:

1. Melt the suet in the saucepan over low heat. Stir so it does not burn.

2. Add the remaining ingredients. Stir again.

3. Remove from heat. Let cool.

4. Refrigerate until firm and serve on a bird feeder.

Did it seem funny to add sand? Birds need grit to help them digest their food.

Match these birds to the descriptions on page 32.

WHO WANTS A WHITE ELEPHANT?

In Siam (now called Thailand), elephants were used to do heavy work. Most elephants were gray. Only a few elephants were white. These elephants were thought to be too special to work. All white elephants were given to the king.

An elephant is expensive to keep because it eats large amounts of food. Since a white elephant did not do work, it was therefore just an expensive pet.

The king of Siam decided to give his white elephants to people he did not like. The people had to take a gift from the king, but a white elephant was a gift that no one really wanted.

Can you find your way through the white elephant?

Name _____

WHOSE FOOT IS THAT?

Animal feet are specialized to do whatever an animal must do to find food and protect itself.

A mountain goat's hooves curve in and have sharp edges. This kind of hoof acts like a suction cup as the mountain goat climbs on narrow ledges. Jumping animals such as rabbits have large back feet which act like a spring-board.

A bear, a cat and many other animals have paws. Put the heel of your hand on the table and press your thumb against your hand. Put your finger-tips on the table. This is what it is like to have a paw.

What animal do you think made each of these footprints?
Put the number of the tracks next to the picture of the animal that made them.

SWAMP MASTER

Color the alligator lightly with a green crayon. Then go over it again with brown. Color the eyes yellow.

The American alligator can grow to be over three meters long. It does not move well on land, but it swims very well. With only its eyes and nostrils above the water, an alligator can swim close to what it wants to catch without being seen.

An alligator is always hungry. It will eat almost anything, even rocks and bottles. It would rather eat fish, turtles, or water birds. With 180 teeth, the alligator has no trouble getting something to eat.

YOU CAN MAKE YOUR OWN SWAMP MASTER

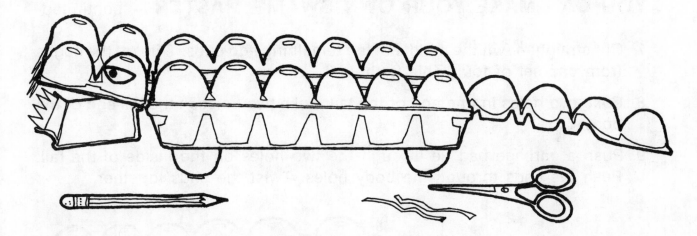

You will need: two styrofoam egg cartons, scissors, a pencil, eight garbage bag ties, a marking pen, white construction paper, and tape.

Directions:

1. Cut across one carton to separate four egg cups.

 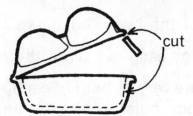 

2. Trim off the sides and edges. This is the head.

3. With a pencil point, poke four holes in the bend of the head.

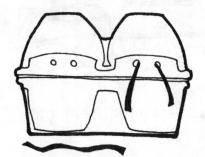 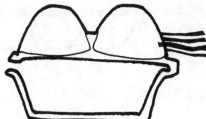 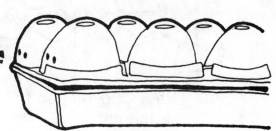

4. Turn the uncut carton so that the flat cover is down. This is the body. Use the pencil to poke four holes in one end of the carton.

5. Open the carton. Slide a garbage bag tie through two of the holes in the head. Push the ends through two of the holes in the body. Twist the ends together on the inside of the body.

6. Do this with the other two holes in the head and body.

YOU CAN MAKE YOUR OWN SWAMP MASTER — continued

7. Cut straight down the middle of the remaining egg cups. Trim off the edges from one set of four. This is the tail.

8. Poke two holes in one end of the tail. Poke two holes in the tail end of the body.

9. Push a garbage bag tie through the two holes on the inside of the tail. Push the ends through the body holes. Twist the ends together.

10. On the flat cover of the body, poke two holes where each leg will be.

11. Use one egg cup for each leg. Trim the edges.

12. Poke two holes in the very bottom of each cup. Push one tie through each leg and into the body holes. Twist the ends together inside the body.

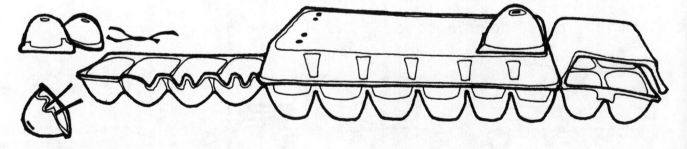

13. Use a marking pen to add eyes. Cut teeth out of paper and tape them into the mouth.

GETTING TO KNOW ME

BACKGROUND

Young people are busy establishing a reference bank of memories and experiences that their brain will relate to when analyzing new situations in the future. Everything has to be touched, looked at, and sniffed, and there may even be a continuing desire to put unknowns into the mouth.

While smelling and tasting have to be carefully supervised because they can be dangerous, it is exciting for students to explore how their body's specialized sense organs function. Understanding can lead to a more meaningful use of these important receptors.

The skin is the center for the sense of touch. Our touch receptors are about three centimeters apart on most parts of our body. On areas designed for touching, such as the fingertips, the touch receptors are very close together.

To test this, spread apart the points of a hairpin, and touch your arm and your fingertip with it. How many points do you feel? Now press the points close together and repeat the test. How many points do you feel? You will feel two points both times on your fingertip but only one point on your arm on the second test.

Our skin is also a good temperature tester. This sense can be tricked because it is a relative sense. We relate environmental temperature to the differences between it and our skin temperature. If our skin is hot, something warm may feel cool.

It is important to be able to make sounds and to be able to hear sounds. Air is forced up through the *larynx* — part of the throat — to make sound. Band-like vocal cords in the larynx are controlled by muscles. Loudness depends on the force of the moving air. Pitch is determined by the number of vibrations per second. In the human voice, pitch is determined by the length and thickness of the vocal cords, and by how tightly they are stretched by the muscles. The longer the cords, the lower is the sound produced. Scientists have discovered that for us to hear a sound that we call middle C, the air must vibrate at a rate of 256 times per second.

These vibrating waves of air are funneled through the outer ear. A membrane called the *eardrum* passes the vibrations on to three small bones — *hammer, anvil* and *stirrup* — in the middle ear. The middle ear is connected by the *Eustachian tube* to the throat. Changes in ear pressure are determined by air moving up this tube.

39

The *oval window* is another membrane that vibrates like a drum head. The inner ear has a shell-shaped organ — the *cochlea* — that is filled with fluid and many nerve endings. As the oval window moves in response to the transmitted vibrations, the fluid moves. Depending on which nerves are touched by the fluid, different electrical signals are sent to the brain.

Our sense of balance is also determined by the movement of the fluid in the cochlea. Balance, like coordination, is improved by practice and experience.

Besides being aware of their environment, young people are also growing. The human body grows in spurts. Just as growth does not occur steadily, neither do all body parts grow at the same time. Feet may get bigger before legs get longer. Realizing the normalcy of this can help to alleviate the feelings of insecurity that accompany growth.

WORD BOX:

object	design	texture
Braille		

LEARNING OBJECTIVES:

1. Students will understand how they can identify objects by touch.

2. Students will understand how different body parts grow in proportion to overall growth.

3. Students will be aware of individual differences.

4. Students will be aware of how they are able to move in a balanced and coordinated way.

5. Students will be aware of the differences in sounds.

PREDICTIONS:

1. Can you tell what something is just by touching it?

2. Will sound move through something solid — a wall, a door, a metal table?

3. Which will make a higher sound, a jar half full of water or a jar with just a little water in it? Why?

4. Do you think that sound will travel better over a tight nylon line or over a sagging nylon line? Why?

DISPLAY AND BULLETIN BOARD IDEAS:

1. Get a large shallow box. Cut one hole on each side. Attach old socks to each hole as shown in the directions for making a Discovery Box (p. 45). Push several items inside.

   Invite students to figure out what is in the box, using only their sense of feel. Each day discuss what they thought was there and why they thought that. Show them what was really there. Add new items for the next day.

2. Make a giant ear for the side of the bulletin board. Label the board NOW HEAR THIS. Put up pictures that illustrate sounds such as a dog barking, race cars running on a track, a moving train, or people dancing. Include cards with printed words that illustrate sounds such as *boom, crunch,* and *pop.* Encourage your students to help you add other pictures and word cards.

3. Display the Real Me People that your students can make as an Extra Spark Starter.

EXTRA SPARK STARTER:

1. Make touch pictures: Request donations of fabric scraps, wallpaper, aluminum foil, wax paper, bottle caps, and various odds and ends that have interesting textures.

   Have the students draw a picture. Using a variety of the collected items, have them fill in areas of the picture.

2. Record a variety of sounds, such as an alarm clock and a toaster popping. How many can your students identify?

3. Make a Real Me of each child:
   Let each student in turn lie down on a big piece of white butcher paper while you or another student carefully outline the student's body.

   Students color their own Real Me. They add the clothes, the face, and the hair. It's nice to have a full-length mirror available during this time.

   Students enjoy creating a life-size duplicate and these doubles are great for parents' open house. Sit each paper child (with the help of a little tape) in the real child's seat. Display the student's work on the desk.

MATERIALS NEEDED:

Shoeboxes
Pencil
Centimeter ruler
Scissors
Old socks
Electrical tape
Empty cans (at least 2 for every 2 students)

White paper
Glue
Metric tape measure or 1 meter of string and a metric ruler
Crayons
Nail
Nylon fish line

Tape
Large wood block
Metal pan
Hardcover book
Quart jars
Metal spoon
Hammer
Buttons (at least 2 for every 2 students)

ADDITIONAL SOURCES: FILMSTRIPS

Discovering Your Senses. Grades 1-3. Set of 6 filmstrips and sound. Coronet.

Slim Goodbody: Your Body, Health and Feelings. Primary and intermediate level. Multi-media kit. SVE-Society For Visual Education, Inc.

Your Senses and How They Help You. Grades K-4. Set of 2 filmstrips and sound. National Geographic Society.

ANSWERS:

Ask students to use complete sentences when answering thought questions.

p. 45: Answers will vary.

p. 46: Answers will vary.

p. 47: The word is hello.

p. 48: Answers will vary.

p. 49: Answers will vary.

p. 52: Answers will vary.

p. 53: 1. the metal
      2. the metal
      3. the metal

p. 56: 1. Answers may vary but generally will be very well. With a three-meter line, the sound vibrations will travel very well providing the line is pulled tight.

2. Answers may vary but generally will be only a little. Sound vibrations can't travel well on a sagging line.

3. Answers may vary but generally will be clearly but soft.
If the line is tight, the vibrations should travel well.
If the line touches anything as it turns the corner, the vibrations will be weakened or stopped.

4. and 5. Answers will vary. Check for logical and realistic ideas and results.

EVALUATION:

Match the beginning half of each sentence on the left to the last half of each sentence on the right. Draw a line to connect the parts together.

1. Sound is really　　　　　　　　　　　　　to your throat.

2. Your Eustachian tube　　　　　　　　　through the larynx.
connects your ear

3. When you talk, air is forced　　　　　　the lower the sound is.

4. The more water there is in a glass,　　　waves of moving air.

5. Your body parts grow　　　　　　　　at different speeds.

Number in order the steps in making a Tin Can Telephone.

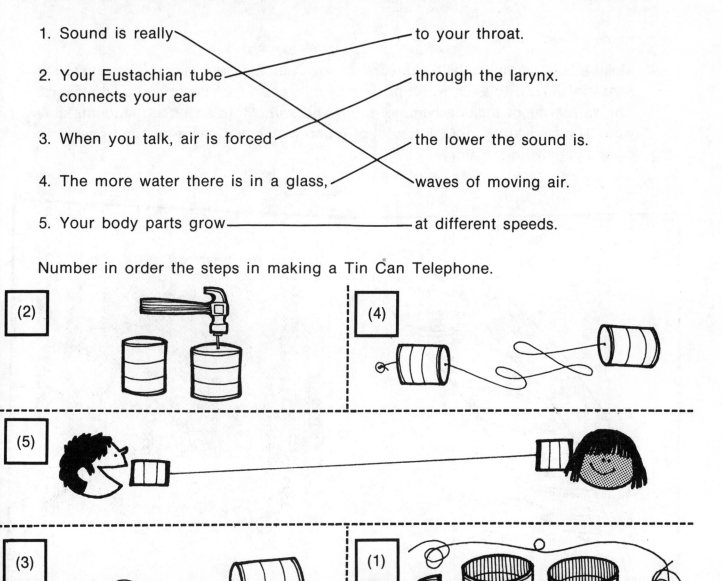

EXTENDED LEARNING:

1. Each person has his or her own space inside a hula hoop or a taped area. Play music (some rock, some classical, some blues). The students move to the music in any way they want to inside their space.

2. Find out more about the human body. Check your library for books about the senses and the human body. Arrange a display of these or read several aloud.

3. Have a visit from a dentist or a dental hygienist.

4. Make a radio play with lots of sound effects. Record this on a tape recorder. Use as many student actors and sound effects people as possible. Then listen to the results.

5. Make a touch book:

Make a book complete with a decorated cover. Include words that illustrate touch sensations. Next to each word, paste a sample of an item described by that word. The words might include *bumpy, rough* and *soft.* More advanced students may want to write a story including a lot of touch words and paste things to feel right on the page with the story.

CAN YOU TELL WHAT SOMETHING IS BY TOUCHING IT?

You will need: a shoebox, a pencil, a ruler, scissors, an old sock and electrical tape.

Directions:

1. Remove the box lid.

2. Use the pencil and ruler to draw a rectangle big enough for your hand to fit through on one end of the box. Cut out the hole.

3. Cut the toe off the sock.

4. Fit the cut-off end of the sock inside the hole and tape it to the box.

5. Have a friend put something into the box and then put on the lid.

6. Slide your hand through the sock until you can touch the object.

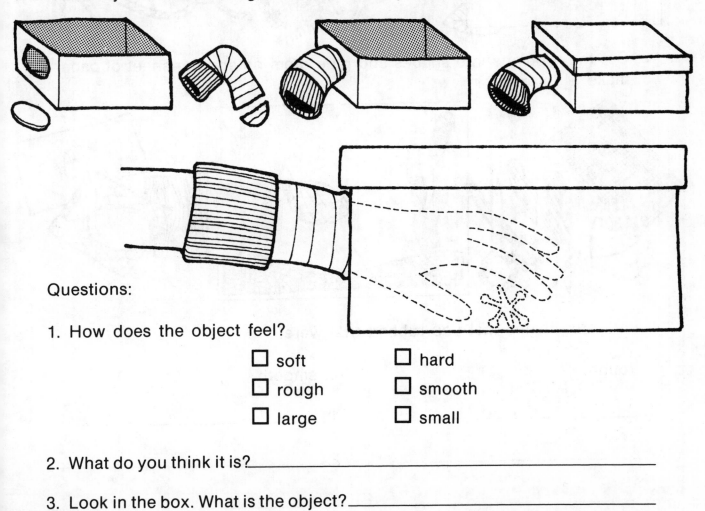

Questions:

1. How does the object feel?

☐ soft ☐ hard

☐ rough ☐ smooth

☐ large ☐ small

2. What do you think it is?_____

3. Look in the box. What is the object?_____

Name_____

FUN SPOT

You can make a texture rub picture.

You will need: white paper, a soft pencil, scissors and glue.

Directions:

1. Put a sheet of paper over what you want to rub. Make rubbings of as many different things as you can.

2. Cut the rubbings into shapes and glue them on another sheet of paper to make a design.

Name three things that you rubbed that were:

rough   smooth

1._____   1._____

2._____   2._____

3._____   3._____

Name _____

KEEPING IN TOUCH

People who can not see can read with their fingers. In the 1800's, a Frenchman named Louis Braille invented a special alphabet for blind people.

This is the Braille alphabet. Put this paper over a magazine or a pad of paper. Press straight down — hard — on each dot with the point of a ball point pen or a pencil with a round point. Be careful not to tear the paper. Then turn the paper over, close your eyes and run your fingers over the raised bumps.

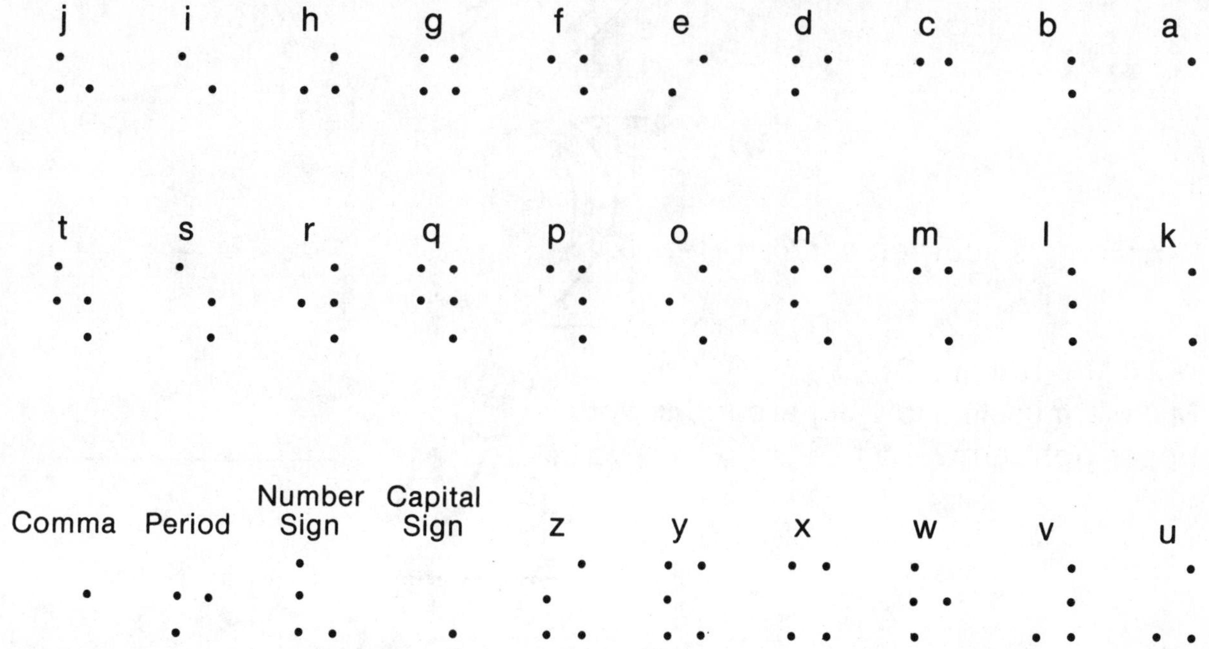

j   i   h   g   f   e   d   c   b   a

t   s   r   q   p   o   n   m   l   k

Comma Period Number Sign Capital Sign z y x w v u

The capital sign before a letter makes it a capital. The number sign before a set of dots makes them a number instead of a letter. There are also 189 special word symbols.

Press these dots, turn the paper over and touch. What is this word?

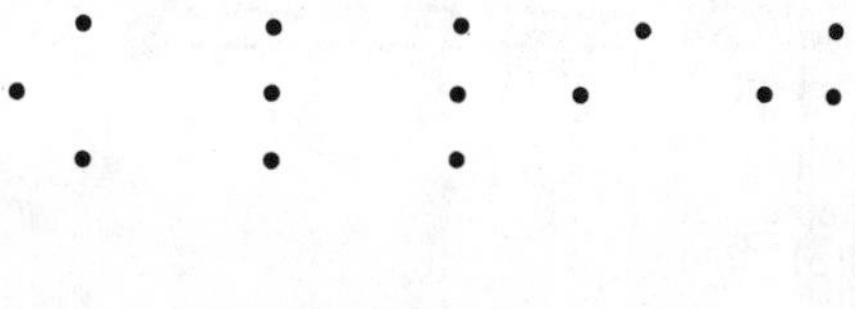

_____

Name _____

HOW BIG AM I?

You will need: a metric tape measure or one meter of string and a metric ruler.

Measure these parts of your body with the metric tape measure. If you do not have a tape measure, measure with the string. Then lay the string on the ruler. Write each measurement on the blank.

1. How long is your right thumb?  _____

2. How long is your left ear?  _____

3. Make a muscle. How big around is your upper right arm?  _____

4. How long is the big toe on your left foot? _____

5. How long is your right foot? 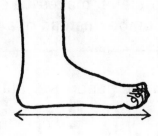 _____

6. How tall are you?  _____

Name _____

HAND SPAN

You will need: a piece of white paper, a pencil, a centimeter ruler, a red crayon and a blue crayon.

Directions:

1. Press your hand on the piece of white paper. Spread your fingers as far apart as you can. Draw around your fingers.

2. Use a centimeter ruler to measure straight from the tip of your little finger to the tip of your thumb. How big is your hand span?

_____

3. Measure the hand span of five boys and five girls in your class. Write their names and their hand spans on the chart.

BOYS	HAND SPAN	GIRLS	HAND SPAN

4. Use a red crayon to circle the biggest hand span. Use a blue crayon to circle the smallest hand span.

HAND-MADE ANIMALS

Your hand can be a swan, a turkey, a dog's head and a fish.

Trace around your hand on pieces of white paper using the patterns shown on this page. Then color in your hand-made animals.

Can you think of any other animals that your hand could become?

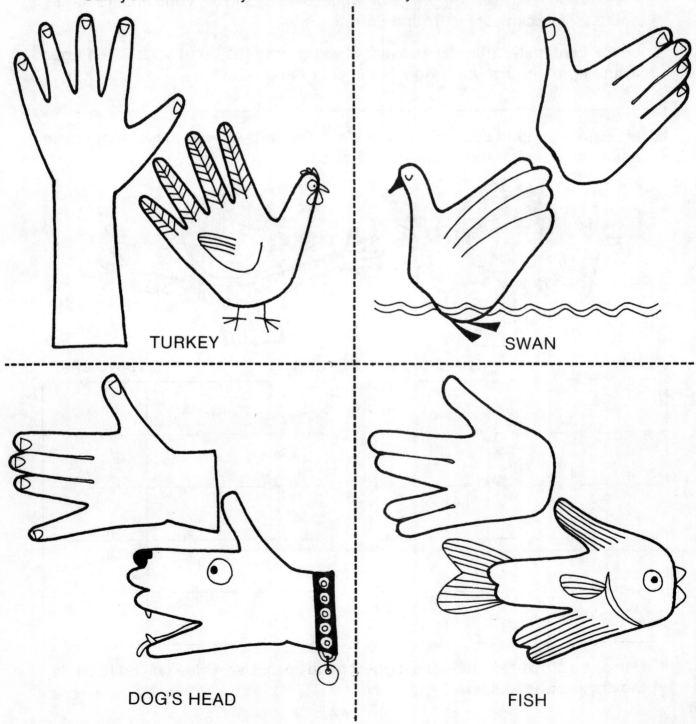

TURKEY

SWAN

DOG'S HEAD

FISH

50

Name _____

HANDS UP

Find words that are things you can do with your hands. Draw a line around each word. Use the Clue Box to help you.

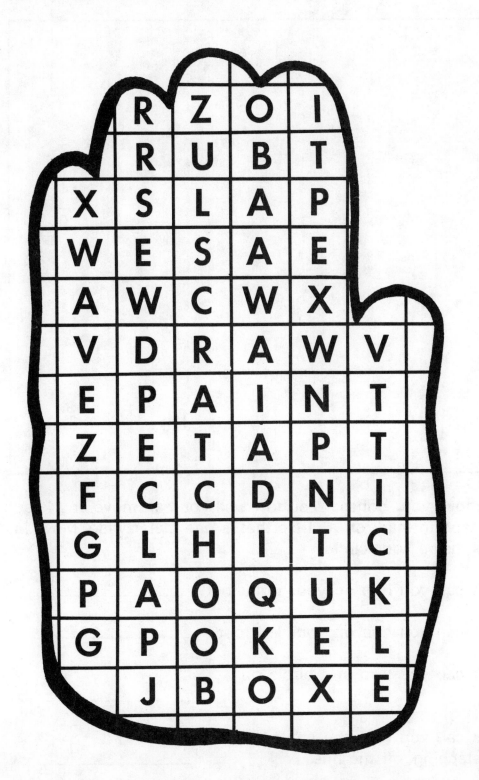

CLUE BOX

SLAP
WAVE
PAT
RUB
DRAW
PAINT
BOX
TAP
SCRATCH
HIT
TICKLE
POINT
POKE
CLAP

KEEP ON MOVING!

Your bones give your body its shape. Can you think what your body would look like without any bones? Draw a picture of you without any bones.

Your muscles move your bones. Test how well you can move and keep your balance. Use tape to mark off a circle that is one meter wide. Move in each of these ways inside your circle.

1. How many times can you hop on your right foot? _____

2. How many times can you hop on your left foot? _____

3. How many times can you turn in a circle on
   one foot?   _____

4. How many times can you walk the circle on your
   tiptoes without stepping off the line?   _____

HOW ARE SOUNDS DIFFERENT?

You will need: a large block of wood, a metal pan and a hardcover book.

Directions:

1. Put your ear against the block of wood. Knock on the wood.

2. Put your ear against the metal pan. Knock on the metal.

3. Put your ear against the book cover. Knock on the cover.

Questions:

1. Which made the highest sound?

   ☐ the wood   ☐ the metal   ☐ the book cover

2. Which made a ringing sound?

   ☐ the wood   ☐ the metal   ☐ the book cover

3. Which had the sound go on after you stopped knocking?

   ☐ the wood   ☐ the metal   ☐ the book cover

MAKE YOUR OWN KIND OF MUSIC

You will need: three quart jars, a metal spoon and water.

Directions:

1. Fill one jar half full of water. Tap it with the spoon. It should make a deep sound. If it does not, add more water.

2. Fill the second jar a little less than half full. Tap it. The sound should be higher than the first jar. If it is not, pour out a little water.

3. The last jar should have just a little water in the bottom. Tap it. It should sound higher than the other two jars.

4. Number the jars as shown in the picture.

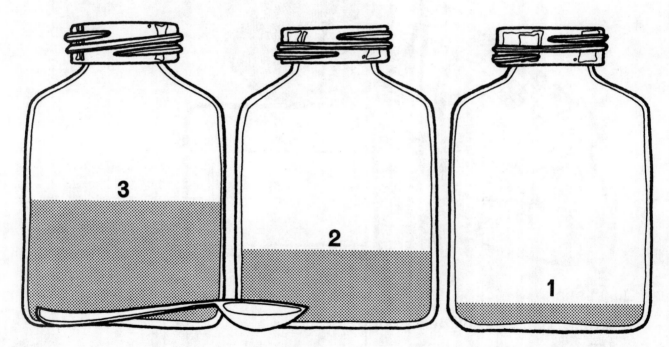

5. You can play "Mary Had a Little Lamb" by following this pattern.

1, 2, 3, 2 — 1, 1, 1 —

2, 2, 2 — 1, 1, 1 —

1, 2, 3, 2, — 1, 1, 1 —

1, 2, 2, 1, 2, 3

Name _____

MAKE YOUR OWN TIN CAN TELEPHONE

You will need: two clean, empty cans with one end open, a nail, a hammer, three meters of nylon fish line, two buttons and a friend.

Directions:

1. Put the nail on the outside of the can bottom. Use the hammer to punch a small hole in each can bottom.

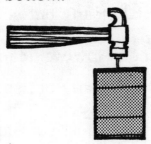

2. Thread one end of the nylon line through one can and tie it to a button on the open end of the can.

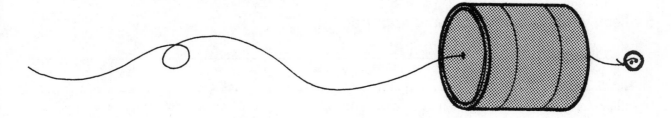

3. Thread the other end of the nylon line through the other can and tie it to the other button.

4. Have your friend take one can and walk away until the line is tight.

5. While your friend talks, hold the open end of your can to your ear.

Name _____

MAKE YOUR OWN TIN CAN TELEPHONE — continued

Questions:

1. How well can you hear your friend?

   ☐ only a little   ☐ clearly but soft   ☐ very well

2. Try again with the line not pulled tight. How well can you hear your friend?

   ☐ only a little   ☐ clearly but soft   ☐ very well

3. Try listening around a corner. How well can you hear your friend?

   ☐ only a little   ☐ clearly but soft   ☐ very well

4. Tell another way that you could test your telephone.

   _____

   _____

5. Test your idea. Tell what happened.

   _____

   _____

FORCES

BACKGROUND

There are many kinds of forces around us and acting on us all the time. Forces may stop or start action. Forces may bend, stretch, twist or even break things. Forces may change the direction or the speed of movement. Forces may change the motion of an object or they may change the object itself.

A force is a push or a pull on an object or person. If a push or a pull moves an object, work is said to be done.

Combined effort can make work easier. Several people, animals, or machines exerting the same kind of force — push or pull — on an object can move more weight with less effort.

Effort can even become combined if a single object can offer many points of support. A single thin string can't support a heavy wooden board. However, if the string is looped around the board and an area of support as shown in the picture, the string can support the wooden board.

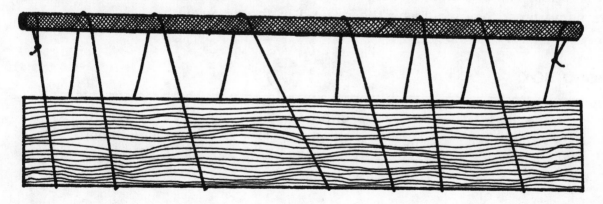

The string is able to pull the board's weight in several places at the same time. The weight is therefore not as great on any one spot. Combined effort is also gained when strands of fibers or paper strips are layered together, twisted together, or rippled, as in corrugated cardboard.

Objects may have more than one force acting on them at one time. What happens to the object depends on which force is stronger.

One force that is constantly applying pressure is *gravity*. The law of gravity as originally stated by Sir Isaac Newton is, "Every body has a pull. The bigger the body, the bigger the pull."

The earth is constantly pulled by the sun. Only the rapid spinning-away motion of the earth keeps us from being pulled into the sun. The spinning-away force is called *centrifugal force.*

The earth is bigger than any person or thing on its surface. Therefore, it pulls everything on the earth toward its own center.

While a pushing or pulling force is acting on an object or person, friction is resisting movement. When something rubs together, this rubbing is called *friction.* Rubbing your hands together creates friction. Tires rubbing on the road create friction. An airplane moving through air molecules — particles of air — creates friction.

Friction can cause heat, slow down movement, or wear away part of an object. Grease and oil are added to reduce friction. Ball bearings — metal spheres — are used to prevent machine parts from rubbing together. Things are streamlined — designed to slice through air or water — to reduce friction.

Galileo Galilei, experimenting long ago in Italy, discovered that as long as objects are the same size and have the same shape, the frictional resistance will be the same despite a difference in weight. For example, if you dropped a golf ball and a solid gold ball of exactly the same size and shape from the top of a tall building at the same time, they would hit the ground at the same time.

WORD BOX:

gravity	effort	pressure
experiment	friction	engineer

LEARNING OBJECTIVES:

1. Students will be able to identify the major forces acting upon objects and people.

2. Students will be able to demonstrate that weight has force.

3. Students will be able to predict the changes that will occur if one of two or more opposing forces is eliminated.

4. Students will understand how gravity affects objects and people.

5. Students will be able to predict how friction will affect an object and suggest ways to overcome friction.

PREDICTIONS:

1. If a ball is tossed into the air, do you think it will come back down? Why?

2. Which will move more weight, one bulldozer or two bulldozers? Why?

3. Which way do you think you could move more weight, by pushing or by pulling? Why?

4. Which do you think can hold more weight, a thread, a string, or a rope?

DISPLAY AND BULLETIN BOARD IDEAS:

1. Divide a bulletin board or display area into two sections. Label one PUSH and the other PULL. Put up pictures that illustrate things being pushed or pulled. Encourage your students to add other pictures.

2. Make a display showing a construction scene. Include a bulldozer, a jackhammer, a wrecking ball, and a crane lifting steel beams. Label the area with the question, "Which machines are pushing and which are pulling?"

3. Make a giant crossword puzzle with words that are push or pull machines such as *tugboat, snowplow* or *train.* Write interesting clues. For younger students, fill in some letters in advance.

Allow students to work on the puzzle as they think they know an answer. Ask students to sign their name or initials on the word that they fill in. For neatness, you may want to approve your student's answers before they write them on the puzzle.

EXTRA SPARK STARTER:

1. Play "Push-Pull":

Divide the class into two teams. Have cards saying either PUSH or PULL and the name of a machine. The teams alternate play. One person on each team draws a card. In pantomime, that person must then act out what that machine does. Each team guesses its own team's actions. The team gets two points for guessing PUSH or PULL and another five points for guessing what the machine is. Set a time limit on guessing to keep play moving.

2. Make push-pull paper chains:

Divide the class into small groups — about five or six people in a group. Give each group paper, scissors, glue, and marking pens or crayons. Give each group two starting paper loops — one that says PUSH and one that says PULL.

Each group makes more loops to add onto each starting ring. Before gluing the new loop together, they must print on it the name of something that pushes or pulls.

Set a time limit. The team with the longest chain of correct loops wins. Offer a special privilege as a reward. Hang the chains down in vertical rows on a display area. Besides being attractive, they will provide a reference source for other work.

MATERIALS NEEDED:

Crayons	Steel ball bearings	Glass marbles
Corks	Carbon paper	Scissors
Glue	Corrugated cardboard	Half-pint milk cartons
Small stones	Balloons	Thread
String	Rope	Notebook paper
		Pencil

ADDITIONAL SOURCES: BOOKS

DeVries, Leonard. The Second Book of Experiments. The Macmillan Co., 1968.

Goldstein-Jackson, Kevin. Experiments With Everyday Objects. Prentice-Hall, Inc., 1978.

Renner, Al G. How To Build A Better Mousetrap Car. Dodd, Mead & Co., 1977.

Vivian, Charles. Science Experiments & Amusements For Children. Dover Publications, 1963.

Wyler, Rose. What Happens If . . ? Walker and Co., 1974.

ADDITIONAL SOURCES: FILMSTRIPS

Matter and Energy. Primary and intermediate level. Set of 6 filmstrips and sound. SVE-Society For Visual Education.

Science and Imagination. Grades 1-5. Multimedia kit. Coronet.

ANSWERS:

Ask students to answer thought questions in complete sentences.

p. 63: 1. PUSH   3. PULL
        2. PULL   4. PUSH
Students' examples will vary.

p. 64: 1. ↑   3. →   5. ↘
        2. ←   4. →   6. ↖
Number six shows a force that is not moving anything.
The mule may move. The rope may break. The clown may fall down.

p. 65: 1. Red →   3. Blue ←   5. Blue ↑
        2. Red →   4. Yellow ↓
Students' answers will vary.

p. 66: The weight of the object made the difference. More weight has more force.
       6. A heavy object has more force than a light object.

p. 67: 1. A space was pressed down.
        2. A hole was made in the cardboard.
        3. There was less pressure on the point than on the eraser.   False.
        4. In the challenge picture, the force made less pressure on the head of the
           tack.

p. 68: 1. Wind, gravity, person holding the string.
        If the wind stopped, the kite would fall. If gravity stopped, the kite would float
        up. If the person holding the string let go, the kite would blow away.
        2. Trees, gravity, weight of person.

p. 69: 2. How did the wad fall? fast
        4. How did it fall? floated down
        5. Which hits the floor first? wad

p. 70: B is faster.

p. 71: 1. Push   2. Pull
        3. Streamlined   4. Bearings
        5. Friction   6. Turbine
        7. Engineer   8. Effort
        9. Combined   10. Force

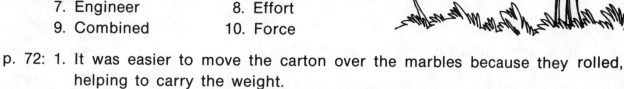

p. 72: 1. It was easier to move the carton over the marbles because they rolled,
           helping to carry the weight.

p. 73: Students should predict a rope can withstand more force. The braided and
       twisted strands of a rope mean that there is combined effort.

       Students' ideas, list of materials, methods, and results will vary. Check for
       thoughtful, logical responses.

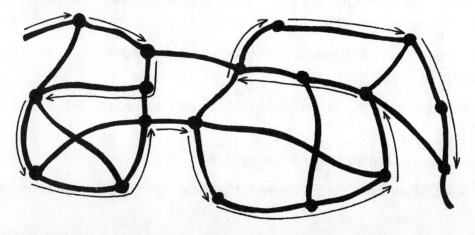

EVALUATION:

Read each statement. Put an *F* next to each sentence that is false and *T* next to each sentence that is true.

1. A force is often a push or pull on something. (T)

2. Combined effort means more people can move less weight. (F)

3. Gravity is the force that pushes everything away from the earth's center. (F)

4. Friction is caused by things rubbing together. (T)

5. Friction speeds things up. (F)

Make an *X* in the box next to the response that best answers each question.

6. Which will hit the ground first if they are dropped together?

   ☒ a paper wad   ☐ a sheet of paper

7. Which is stronger?

   ☐ a thread   ☐ a string   ☒ a rope

8. Where does force have more pressure?

   ☒ on a small area   ☐ on a big area

9. Which has more force?

   ☒ a steel ball bearing   ☐ a glass marble

10. Why are machine parts oiled?

   ☒ to help stop friction   ☐ to hold parts together

EXTENDED LEARNING:

1. Have students plan and design paper airplanes. Plan a contest. Award certificates or ribbons for design, straightest flight to ground target, and longest flight.

2. Can students design shock-absorbent packages so that eggs could be dropped without breaking?

3. Have students plan, design, and build paper bridges. Which can support the most weight?

4. Find out more about Galileo and his experiments.

5. Design and build small race cars. Whose design can overcome friction the best?

Name _____

WHAT IS A FORCE?

Forces are pushes or pulls. They act on everything around us all the time. Which pictures show pushing? Which pictures show pulling? Write PUSH or PULL under each picture.

1.

_____

3.

_____

2.

_____

4.

_____

Name two more actions that show a pushing force and two that show a pulling force.

PUSH

1. _____

2. _____

PULL

1. _____

2. _____

Name _____

WHAT IS THE DIRECTION OF THE FORCE?

Forces may start or stop action. Forces may change the direction or the speed at which things move. Use a red crayon or pencil. Draw an arrow to show the direction of the force acting on each numbered part of the picture.

Which picture shows a force that is not moving anything? _____

What may happen in that picture? _____

_____

HOW STRONG IS THE FORCE?

Some forces are much stronger than others. Use a red crayon to show a strong force, a blue crayon to show a medium force and a yellow crayon to show a weak force. Draw an arrow to show the direction of the force acting on each numbered part of the picture.

What is something that you do that takes a lot of force?

_____

_____

What is something that you do that takes only a little force?

_____

_____

Name _____

DOES WEIGHT HAVE FORCE?

You will need: a steel ball bearing, a glass marble, a cork, one sheet of note-book paper, one sheet of carbon paper, a pencil, scissors and glue.

Directions:

1. Put the notebook paper on a smooth, flat floor. Put the carbon paper under the notebook paper with the carbon side up.

2. Roll the steel ball bearing across the paper. Pick up the paper, turn it over, and mark that path number one.

3. Roll the marble and the cork across the paper and number their tracks.

4. Look at the tracks. Your pushing force was the same. What made the

   difference? _____

   _____

5. Cut out a square of the notebook paper to show the track of each object and glue it in the frame.

6. A heavy object has

   ☐ more force than a light object.   ☐ less force than a light object.

Name _____

DOES A FORCE HAVE A GREATER PRESSURE ON A SMALL AREA OR A BIG AREA?

Challenge Picture

Circle the picture that shows the way you would push in a tack.

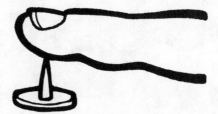   

You will need: a pencil and a piece of corrugated cardboard.

Directions:

1. Hold the pencil with the eraser end on the cardboard. Press down firmly.

2. Turn the pencil over and press down with the point on the cardboard. Try to use the same amount of force as you did before.

Questions:

1. What happened to the cardboard when the eraser was pressed down?

   _____

   _____

2. What happened to the cardboard when the point was pressed down?

   _____

   _____

3. There was less pressure on the point than on the eraser.

   ☐ true   ☐ false

4. In the challenge picture, the force made less pressure on

   ☐ the point of the tack.   ☐ the head of the tack.

Name _____

WHAT IS GRAVITY?

Forces often push or pull on objects and people from more than one direction at the same time. One of the forces pulling on everything on earth is *gravity*. What is gravity?

A long time ago, Sir Isaac Newton was sitting under an apple tree. Suddenly, an apple fell and hit him on the head.

Newton was the first to realize that the earth has a force pulling everything toward its center. This force is what we call gravity.

Below each picture, name two forces acting on the solid black object.

1.

2.

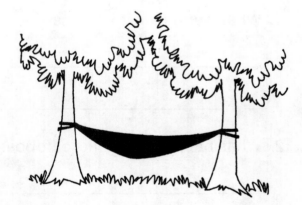

_____   _____

_____   _____

What would happen to the kite if one force stopped? _____

_____

WHAT IS FRICTION?

You will need: two sheets of notebook paper.

Directions:

1. Crush a sheet of notebook paper into a tight ball. Drop it from your hand. Watch it fall to the floor.

2. How did the wad fall?

   ☐ fast   ☐ medium fast   ☐ floated down

3. Drop a sheet of notebook paper. Watch it fall.

4. How did it fall?

   ☐ fast   ☐ medium fast   ☐ floated down

5. Drop the wad and the sheet at the same time from the same height. Which hits the floor first?

   ☐ wad   ☐ sheet

   Everything that moves through the air rubs against the invisible air particles. Friction is this rubbing.

HOW CAN YOU OVERCOME FRICTION?

Engineers are people who design and build things. Engineers who design cars, airplanes and boats work hard to make their designs streamlined. Something that is streamlined will slide through the air with as little friction as possible.

Circle which car you think can travel faster.

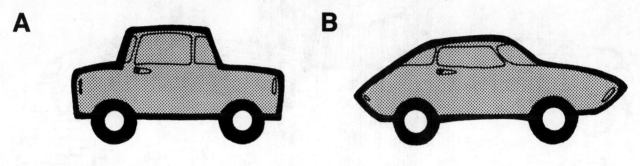

A   **B**

FUN SPOT

Be an engineer. Design a superfast, steamlined car. Draw and color a picture of your car. Give it a name.

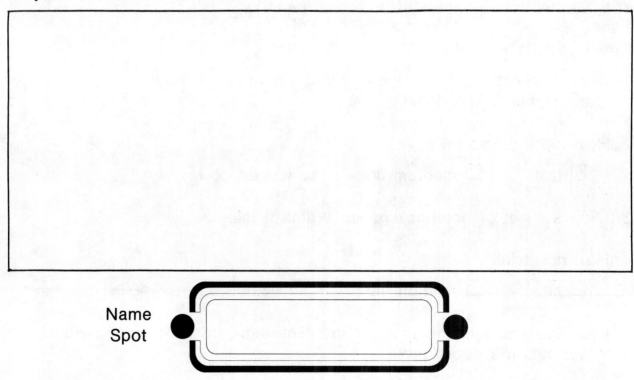

Name
Spot

The fastest car on record was a forty-foot, dart-shaped car driven by Stan Barrett and sponsored by Anheuser-Busch, Inc. It went 739.666 m.p.h. on December 17, 1979.

PUZZLE FUN

Use the clues to help you fill in the crossword puzzle.

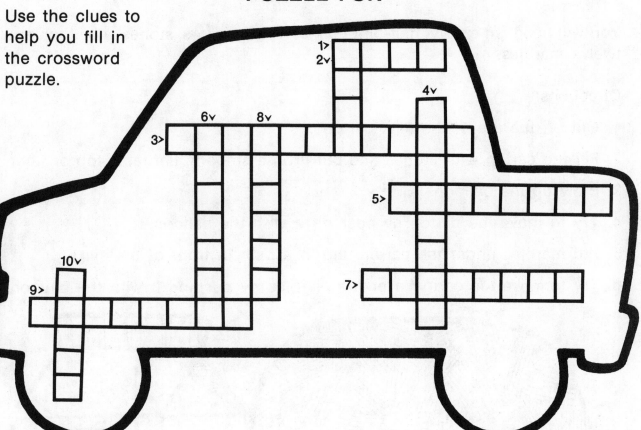

ACROSS

1. A force away from something

3. A shape to help stop friction

5. Things rubbing together

7. A person who designs things

9. One or more people or machines working together

DOWN

2. A force toward something

4. Something round to help machine parts slide together with less friction

6. A machine to use forces to do work

8. The amount of force needed to do work

10. A push or pull on something

CLUE BOX

PUSH	FORCE	FRICTION	BEARINGS
PULL	TURBINE	ENGINEER	EFFORT
	STREAMLINED	COMBINED	

IS THERE ANOTHER WAY TO STOP FRICTION?

You will need: an empty half-pint milk carton, scissors, stones, a balloon and twelve marbles.

Directions:

1. Cut off the top of the milk carton.

2. Fill the carton with stones and put it on a smooth, flat table top or floor.

3. Blow up the balloon.

4. Try to move the carton by pushing it with the balloon.

5. Put marbles under the carton and in a path in front of the carton.

6. Try to move the carton over the marbles by pushing it with the balloon.

Questions:

1. Why do you think it was easier to move the carton over the marbles?

_____

_____

Today most machines use ball bearings to help stop friction. The marbles are like the ball bearings.

Name _____

WHICH IS STRONGER?

Which do you think can withstand more force?

☐ a thread   ☐ a string   ☐ a rope

Here are two ways to find out which is stronger.

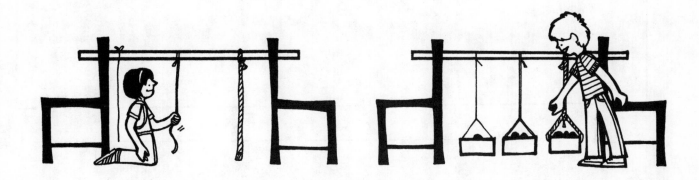

You can use one of these ideas or make up one of your own.

Tell how you will test your prediction.

_____

_____

List the supplies you will need.

_____

_____

Tell how you will do it.

_____

_____

_____

Name _____

WHICH IS STRONGER — continued

Draw a picture of your experiment.

Tell what happened. _____

_____

_____

_____

FUN SPOT

Can you find your way past all the knots? You must touch each knot once, but you may not cross your own path.

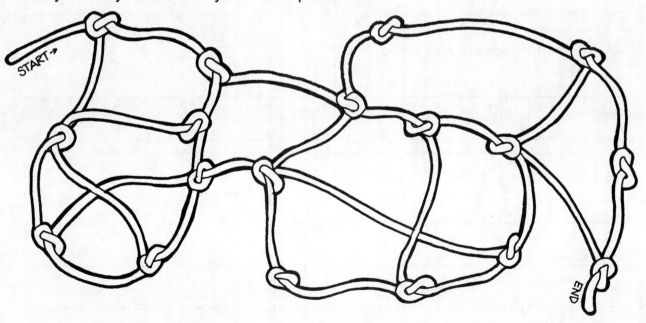

GREEN FRIENDS

BACKGROUND

Green plants are our friends. Only green plants can make their own food. Scientists don't yet know just how green plants do it. They do know that this process — *photosynthesis* — follows this formula:

Sunlight + Chlorophyll + Carbon dioxide + Water = Sugar and Starch + Oxygen.

Chlorophyll is the chemical that makes plants green. Any part of the plant that is green can make food, but the leaves are the main food factories.

Plants have a system of tubes to transport liquids. The *xylem* tubes carry water up to the leaves from the ground. *Phloem* tubes carry food from the leaves down to the stem and roots to be stored.

When you think how tall some plants are, you can see what an amazing system this is. The food moves down mainly by the pull of gravity. Water evaporates from the leaves. This starts a suction force on the water within the plant. Because water molecules tend to cling together, a whole column of water rises in the plant.

When green plants reach a certain size and stage of development, they produce flowers. Some green plants produce two kinds of flowers — one with the male reproductive organs and the other with the female reproductive organs. These plants must depend on insects, birds, or the wind to carry *pollen* — male cells — to the *ovules* — female cells.

In other green plants, the male and female parts are in the same **flower**. The pollen grains unite with the ovule to make a fertile cell — the *seed.* Then the flower withers and the female organ — the ovary — enlarges. The seeds grow and mature.

The ovary both protects the seeds and provides a way for the seeds to be spread. If too many plants grew in the same spot, there would not be enough water, root room, or available soil minerals. Most plants produce many seeds to be sure that at least a few will survive and grow.

In some cases, the ovary develops into a fruit or a vegetable. Animals eat these. The seeds are not digested and are later passed with the animal's wastes. Thus the seeds are both carried to a new location and provided fertilizer to help them grow.

Other seeds are carried to new homes by the wind or by clinging to an animal's fur, as many weed seeds do.

A seed has a tough protective coat. When water enters through a small hole, the coat splits open. The root pushes out first. Then the stem shoves up with the first true leaves. Another miracle of plant growth is that no matter which way the seed is put into the ground, the root will still go down and the stem will push up into the sunlight.

The part of the seed that is food for us is also stored food for the young plant. These structures are called *cotyledons*. They cling to the plant during its first couple of weeks of life. With the help of the cotyledons, the young plants can begin growing without dirt or sunlight — only water is necessary. When the stored food is used up, the plants must have both dirt and sunlight to continue growing.

WORD BOX:

seed	cotyledon	seed coat
embryo	sprout	

LEARNING OBJECTIVES:

1. Students will understand what a seed needs to sprout and how the sprouting begins.

2. Students will be aware of what cotyledons do for the young plant.

3. Students will be able to recognize variations in seeds, the number produced, and the way they are spread.

4. Students will be able to observe carefully and predict results.

PREDICTIONS:

1. What part of the young plant do you think pushes out of the seed first: the root, stem, or leaves?

2. What part of the plant do you think makes seeds?

3. Which do you think has more seeds: an apple, a grape, or an orange? (Cut one of each open to demonstrate results.)

DISPLAY AND BULLETIN BOARD IDEAS:

1. Make a bulletin board showing a common life cycle of a green plant.

   Make a giant flower. Show the seeds developing inside the ovary.
   Show a seed by itself. Then show a seed sprouting.
   Have several increasingly bigger plants.
   Connect all the stages with arrows.

2. Put up a large map of the United States on a bulletin board or display area. Show the state flowers and state trees.

3. Arrange a display of books about plants.

EXTRA SPARK STARTER:

1. Have students bring in a variety of leaves and weeds. Dry and press them between layers of newspaper. Use white glue on colored construction paper to make collages. Display these in the room.

2. Take a walk together around the school grounds. Collect leaves. Look at plants closely. Notice how leaves are arranged on stems and branches. Make rubbings of bark to see the pattern variations. Carefully pull up some weeds and some grass. Look at the roots and notice the differences.

MATERIALS NEEDED:

*Bean seeds or dried seeds	Bowls	Magnifying glass
Tall glasses	Potting soil	Crayons
A variety of seeds	White glue	Apples, dry ears of corn,
Colored construction paper	Pumpkins (at least	and dry pine cones (at
Marking pens	1 for every 2	least 1 of each for
Newspapers	students)	every 2 students)
Knife	Spoon	Pill bottles with lids
		Posterboard

*Dried beans which can be purchased by the bag at grocery stores will sprout and grow well.

ADDITIONAL SOURCES: FILMSTRIPS

Learning About Ecology. Primary and intermediate level. Set of 6 filmstrips and sound. Encyclopedia Britannica Educational Corporation.

Places Where Plants and Animals Live. Grades K-4. Set of 5 filmstrips and sound. National Geographic Society.

The World of Plants. Grades K-4. Set of 5 filmstrips and sound. National Geographic Society.

Ask students to answer thought questions in complete sentences.

ANSWERS:

p. 81: 1. Nothing happened to the bottle that had only seeds.
2. The top popped off (or was pushed up) on the bottle that had both seeds and water.
3. The seeds in the water have gotten larger (swelled). The seed coat is coming off. Some seeds have split open. Evidence of sprouting may already be visible.

p. 82: The thin seed coat __(2)__ covers the seed. A small hole __(1)__ in the seed coat lets water into the seed.

Pull the two halves of the seed apart. The two big parts store food for the young plant. They are called cotyledons __(3)__ . The young plant is called an embryo __(4)__ . It has a root, stem, and leaves.

p. 83: 1. Root.
2. Answers will vary. Generally, it will take 2-7 days for the plant to push through the dirt.
3. Answers will vary. Generally, it will take 10-14 days for the cotyledons to fall off.

p. 84: 1. Bud   3. Stem   5. Root
2. Leaf   4. Cotyledon

p. 85: Answers will vary about the numbers of seeds.
1. The apple falls to the ground and rots. The seeds are then released from the fruit.
2. Plants produce a lot of seeds because then at least a few may survive.

p. 87: Students may need help identifying their trees. Tree books will show tree shape, leaf shape, twig features (for winter identification) and special characteristics. Decorative varieties may need to be identified by experts. Most county agricultural extension agents will help. 4-H groups or local greenhouses can be contacted.

p. 89: 1. Answers will vary.
2. Answers will vary. Generally, the sound will be deeper in the middle or toward the bottom depending on the shape and maturity of the pumpkin.
4. Answers will vary.
6. Answers will vary.

p. 90: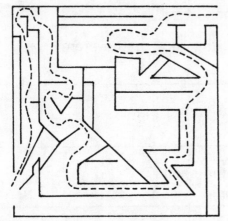

p. 91: This is a saguaro cactus.

TEACHER'S NOTES:

When you are collecting seeds, the dried seeds that you can buy in grocery stores grow very well. Bird seed also can provide a variety of seed types. All seeds sprout much faster if they are soaked in water overnight.

If you plant a variety of seeds, keep in mind that green plants belong to two main groups: monocots and dicots.

The monocots are like grasses and corn. The leaves have parallel veins. The seeds have only one cotyledon and in a number of plants it remains underground.

The dicots are like beans and peas. The leaves are broad with varied patterns of veins. The seeds have two cotyledons, which usually remain attached to the stem for several days to several weeks. In some plants, like the castor bean, they may appear as the first leaves.

EVALUATION:

Use the words in the box at the right to label the parts of the young plant.

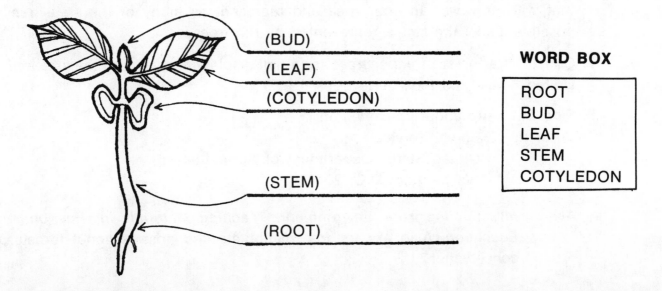

(BUD)

(LEAF)

(COTYLEDON)

(STEM)

(ROOT)

WORD BOX

ROOT
BUD
LEAF
STEM
COTYLEDON

Write a short answer for each question.

1. Which pushes out of the seed first, the root or the stem?

   (root)

2. What does the cotyledon do for the young plant?
   (has stored food)

3. What part of a green plant makes the seeds?
   (flower)

   What are two ways that seeds move to new homes?

4.   (wind — animal's fur — carried and buried by animals)

5.   (water — eaten by animals and passed with wastes)

EXTENDED LEARNING:

1. Find out more about specific plants. Make a class book together. Each person writes a short factual story about one kind of plant and draws and colors a picture of that plant. The book should include a table of contents and possibly a glossary. The book can be displayed in the room and donated to the library.

2. Make terrariums.

3. Visit a botanical garden, a greenhouse, or a florist.

4. Have a visit from a botanist or possibly a forest ranger.

5. Label the trees on the school grounds.

6. With permission from your principal, plan an area where trees can be planted. Have a fund-raising event and arrange for donations. Purchase and plant trees that will grow well in your area and represent as many of the state trees as possible. Label the states represented by the trees.

7. Construct a forest of paper trees for a hall display representing the states of the United States and their state trees.

8. Find out more about conservation.
   Write to: Forest Service
   United States Department of Agriculture
   Washington, D.C. 20402

   Ask for *Investigating Your Environment: Teaching Materials for Environmental Education.* Also ask for free pamphlets and posters about forests and conservation.

Name _____

WHAT IS A SEED?

A seed is like an egg. The hard shell protects the baby chick until it is ready to hatch. Inside the seed coat is a baby plant getting ready to sprout.

 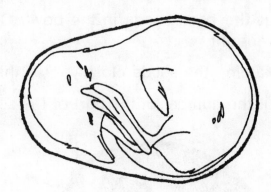

You will need: bean seeds or dried beans and two pill bottles with lids.

Directions:

1. Fill each pill bottle with bean seeds.

2. Pour water into one bottle until it is full.

3. Put the caps on both bottles and let them sit overnight.

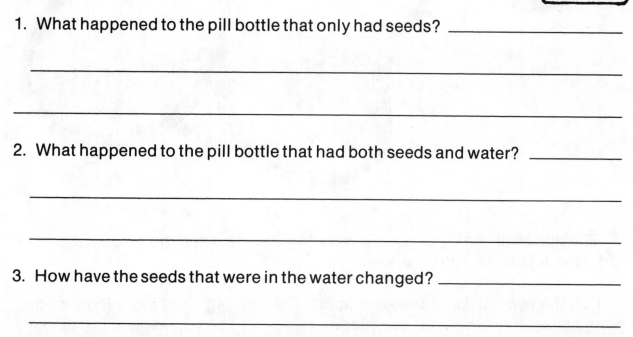

Questions:

1. What happened to the pill bottle that only had seeds? _____

_____

_____

2. What happened to the pill bottle that had both seeds and water? _____

_____

_____

3. How have the seeds that were in the water changed? _____

_____

_____

Name _____

WHAT IS INSIDE A SEED?

You will need: five bean seeds or dried beans, a bowl and a magnifying glass.

Directions:

1. Put the bean seeds in the bowl. Cover them with water and let them sit overnight.

2. Examine the seeds closely. Use the magnifying glass.

3. Put the number of the part of the seed on the blank next to its description.

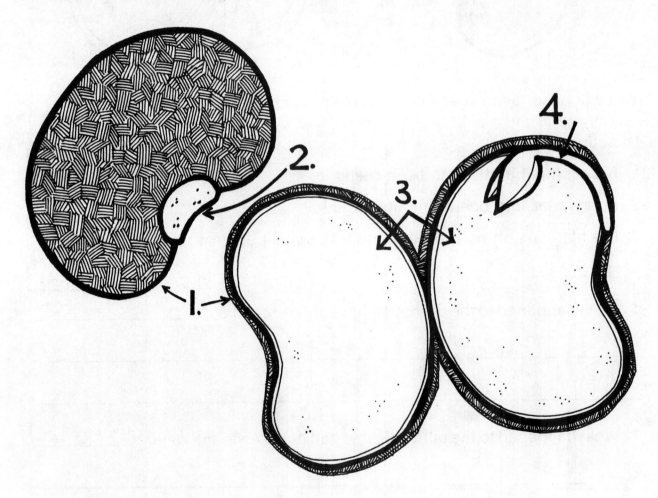

The thin seed coat _____ covers the seed. A small hole _____ in the seed coat lets water into the seed.

Pull the two halves of the seed apart. The two big parts store food for the young plant. They are called cotyledons _____ . The young plant is called an embryo _____ . It has a root, stem and leaves.

Name _____

HOW DO SEEDS BECOME PLANTS?

You will need: a tall glass, potting soil, twelve bean seeds or dried beans and a bowl.

Directions:

1. Put the bean seeds in the bowl, cover with water and let sit overnight.

2. Fill the glass almost to the top with soil.

3. Push the seeds into the dirt close to the glass. Put the glass in a warm spot.

4. Sprinkle the dirt with water as needed to keep it moist.

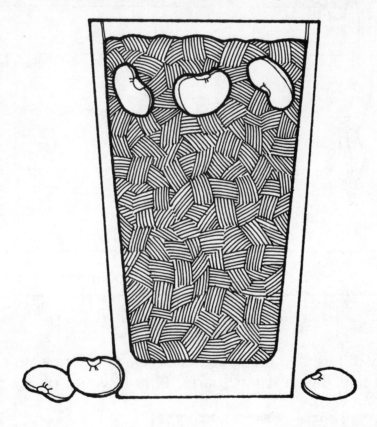

Questions:

1. Which pushes out first, the root or the stem? _____

2. How many days does it take the first young plant to push above the dirt?

_____

3. The cotyledons are on the stem below the leaves. They give the young plant food to begin growing. How many days do the cotyledons remain on the plant before they fall off? _____

Name _____

HOW DO SEEDS BECOME PLANTS — continued

Color the picture to look like your plant. Use the words in the box to name the parts of the plant. Write the names on the lines.

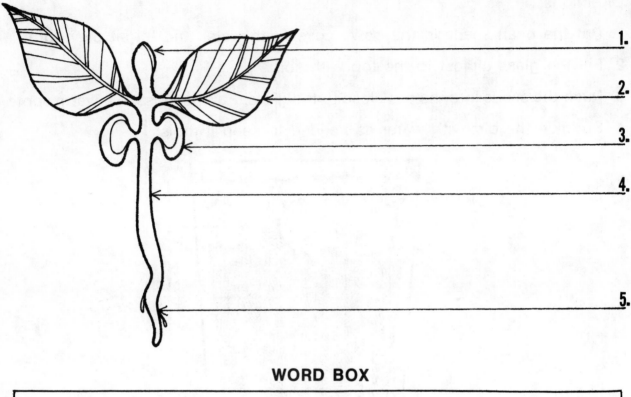

1. _____

2. _____

3. _____

4. _____

5. _____

WORD BOX

root	bud	stem	cotyledon	leaf

FUN SPOT

Collect as many different kinds of seeds as you can. Draw a picture on a piece of posterboard and divide it into parts. Spread white glue on one part at a time.

Put seeds side by side on the posterboard. Plan where you will use different seeds for different colors and appearance.

Name _____

HOW MANY SEEDS DOES A PLANT MAKE?

You will need: an apple, a dry ear of corn, a dry pine cone and a knife.

How many seeds do you think are in an apple? _____
on an ear of corn? _____ in a pine cone? _____

Carefully, cut open the apple and count the seeds. Count the seeds on the ear of corn and the pine cone. Each kernel of corn is a seed. Each part of a pine cone is a seed. Write the number of seeds you find in each.

Apple 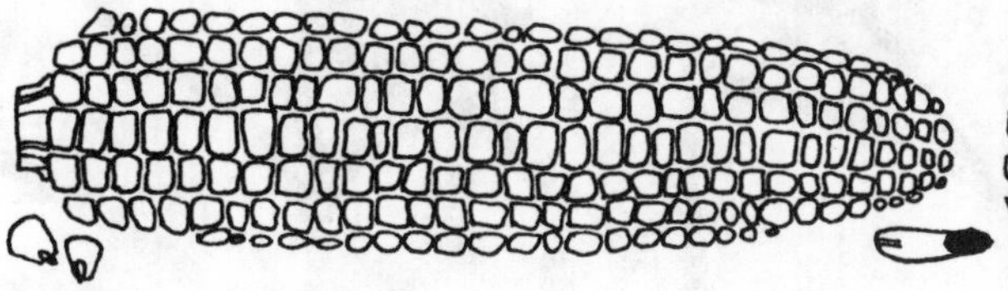   Corn    Pine Cone

_____   _____   _____

Not every apple, ear of corn or pine cone will have the same number of seeds as the ones you counted, but the amount will be nearly the same.

Questions:

1. How do you think the seeds will get out of the apple in order to grow?

_____

_____

2. Why do you think plants produce so many seeds? _____

_____

_____

Name _____

FLOWER POWER

Color each area RED that has the name of a flower.
Color each area GREEN that has the name of a tree.
Color all the other areas YELLOW.

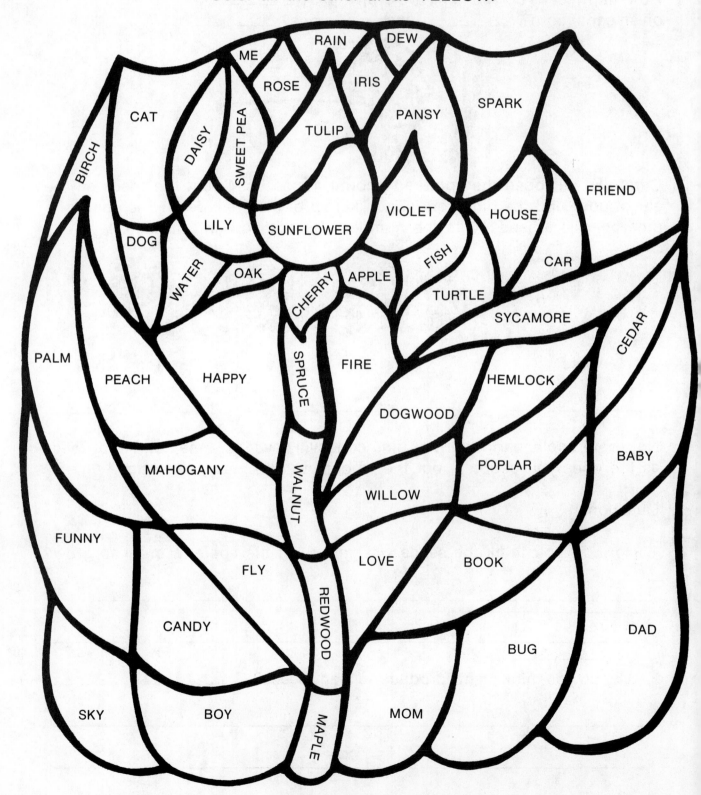

Name _____

ADOPT A TREE

Pick one tree to be your friend for a year. Make a book about your tree. Use colored construction paper for the front and back cover. Put seven pages of notebook paper in your book and staple the pages together. Number the pages. Here is what you should put on each page.

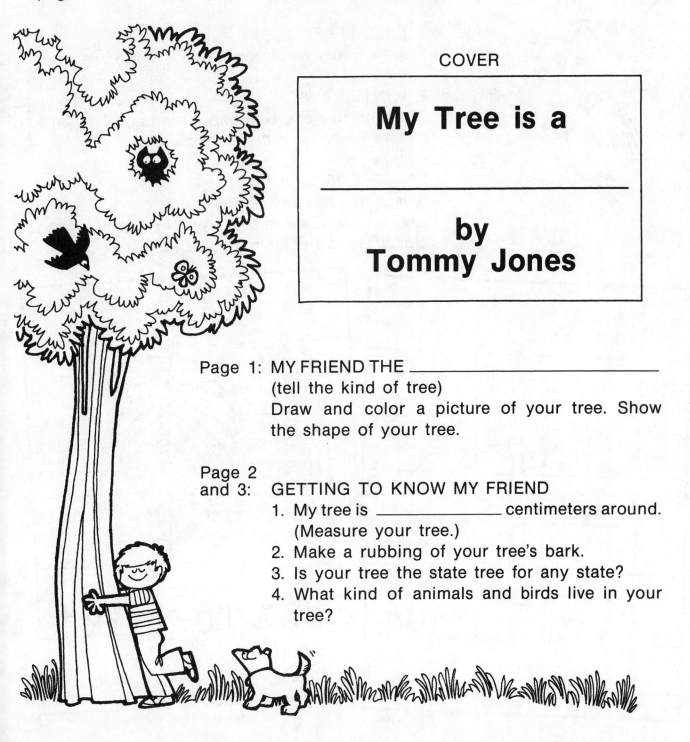

COVER

My Tree is a

_____

by
Tommy Jones

Page 1: MY FRIEND THE _____
(tell the kind of tree)
Draw and color a picture of your tree. Show the shape of your tree.

Page 2 and 3: GETTING TO KNOW MY FRIEND
1. My tree is _____ centimeters around. (Measure your tree.)
2. Make a rubbing of your tree's bark.
3. Is your tree the state tree for any state?
4. What kind of animals and birds live in your tree?

Name _____

ADOPT A TREE — continued

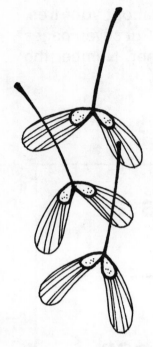

Page 4: A SUMMER LEAF
Press and dry a green leaf from your tree.
Use tape to put it on this page.

Page 5: A FALL LEAF
Press and dry a colored leaf. Tape it to this page.

Page 6: A WINTER TWIG
Break off one end twig about ten to twelve centimeters long. Tape it to this page.

Page 7: MY TREE IS SPECIAL
If your tree has any seeds, cones, or fruit, collect some. Tape some to this page, or if they are too big, draw and color a picture of them.

A winter twig

A summer leaf

Name _____

JACK-O-LANTERN SPECIAL

You will need: a pumpkin, a marking pen, a newspaper, a knife and a spoon. You may need an adult's help.

Directions:

1. Count the lines. How many lines does your pumpkin have? _____

2. Tap your pumpkin with your hand. Where does it make the lowest sound?

   ☐ near the bottom   ☐ in the middle   ☐ near the top

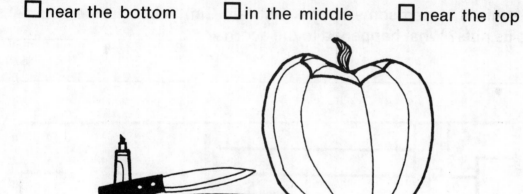

3. Draw a circle around the top of your pumpkin with the pen. Use the knife to cut along this line. Remove the top.

4. How many seeds do you think your pumpkin has? _____

5. Spread out the newspaper. Scoop the seeds out of your pumpkin with the spoon. Put them on the newspaper.

6. Count the seeds. How many seeds are there? _____

7. Use the marking pen to make eyes, a nose and a mouth on your pumpkin.

Name _____

HOW DO PLANTS TRAVEL?

Plants do most of their traveling as seeds. Fruit falls to the ground and rots. The seeds inside the fruit sprout. New plants start to grow.

Animals carry weed seeds in their fur. Animals eat fruits or vegetables but do not digest the seeds. The seeds leave the animal's body with its wastes and start to grow. Wind and water also carry seeds to new homes. Seeds travel so that too many plants will not grow in one spot.

The squirrel buried some acorns last fall. Can you help the squirrel find its way to its nuts? What happened to the acorns? _____

_____

MYSTERY PLANT

Connect the dots to see what the mystery plant looks like. After reading the story, color the picture.

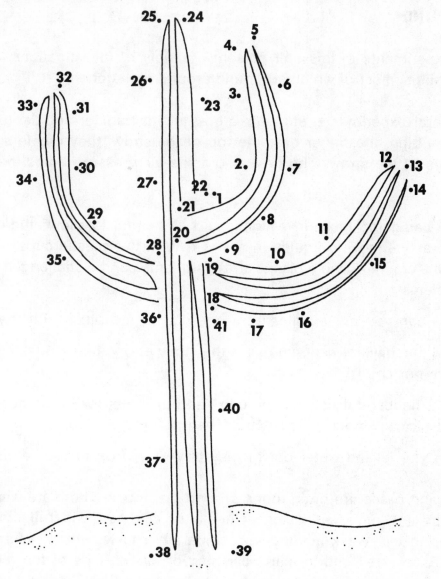

This plant may grow to be eighteen meters tall. It has needles instead of leaves.

It grows in the deserts of the southwestern United States. The roots spread out for almost an acre around the plant. Each root is just below the surface of the soil.

When it does rain, the fleshy stem swells as the water moves up from the roots. The mystery plant can hold 235 gallons of water.

Color the plant green. You may want to add white flowers and red fruit. What plant is this? _____

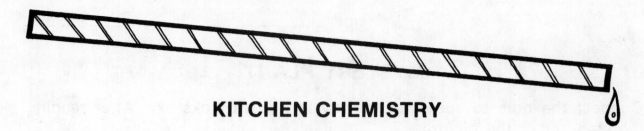

KITCHEN CHEMISTRY

BACKGROUND

The experiments in this unit present a variety of investigations, all done with common things, most of which are found around the kitchen.

In several experiments, students are asked to transfer liquids, using a plastic straw. By putting one finger over the top of the straw, they create an area of less pressure inside the straw. The greater outside air pressure holds the liquid in the straw.

Before beginning these investigations, it is helpful to allow students an opportunity to practice moving liquids in a straw. With two plastic cups — one half-full of water, one empty — and a plastic straw, students can be challenged to investigate these problems:

1. How can you move water from one cup to the other with the straw?

2. How much water can you get in the straw at one time? Sucking on the straw does not count.

3. What happens if you tip the cup and put the straw in the deep water? Can you pick up more or less water than before?

4. Can you let the water out of the straw one drop at a time?

Acids and *bases* are often found around the house. There are weak and strong acids and bases. Some weak acids include citric acid, found in fruit juices, and tannic acid, found in tea. Weak acids give foods a bitter taste. Strong acids are found in batteries. Bases are used in many cleaning products. One of the few bases used in foods is baking soda. Things which are neither an acid nor a base are said to be neutral.

Scientists use either litmus paper or an indicator to show **them** whether something is an acid, a base, or a neutral substance. *Litmus paper* is made from lichens — grayish-green, crusty plants that grow on rocks or tree bark. Blue litmus paper turns pink in an acid and stays blue in a base. Pink litmus paper turns blue in a base and stays pink in an acid. If neither paper changes color, the substance is neutral. If you can get some litmus paper, allow your students to investigate this way of identifying acids and bases.

An *indicator* is a chemical that changes color to show an acid or a base. Phenolphathalein turns bright pink in a base. Phenolphathalein can be purchased, but it is cheaper to mix your own. It is an ingredient in many laxatives. One tablet containing phenolphathalein dissolved in one-fourth cup of rubbing alcohol makes a good indicator. Phenolphathalein remains clear in an acid. Therefore, its one disadvantage is that it cannot be used to distinguish between an acid and a neutral substance.

Grape juice is another indicator. Grape juice is light purple in a neutral substance. As an indicator, grape juice is mixed with water in a ratio of nine parts water to one part grape juice. The indicator turns dark green in a base and light red in an acid. Beet juice and red cabbage juice can be used in the same way.

Emulsions are explored in this unit. In an emulsion, one substance is evenly spread in another substance. When liquids will not mix, the addition of a third substance will help an emulsion form. Oil and water will not mix. When liquid detergent is added, the soap breaks the oil into tiny droplets that become evenly distributed throughout the water. This is how soap helps to remove dirt from cloth.

When working to find out which kind of paper soaks up the most water, *capillary action* is investigated. Water moves through the tiny openings in paper. Because water molecules cling together, a whole column of water moves up the paper.

WORD BOX:

acid	emulsion	rust
base	reaction	indicator
litmus paper	solution	

LEARNING OBJECTIVES:

1. Students will be able to identify acids and bases using an indicator.

2. Students will be able to identify acids and bases using litmus paper.

3. Students will be aware of how soap forms an emulsion.

4. Students will understand how rust forms and be able to suggest ways to stop it.

5. Students will be able to make a prediction and determine how to test their ideas.

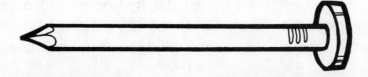

PREDICTIONS:

1. Acids are often found in foods. Bases are often used in cleaning products. Which do you think is an acid, vinegar or ammonia? Why?

2. Since grape juice is an indicator, how do you think it will show an acid and a base?

3. What do you think will happen when the vinegar and baking soda combine?

4. How do you think soap gets dirt out of cloth?

5. Show several kinds of paper towels. Which do you think will soak up the most water? Why?

DISPLAY AND BULLETIN BOARD IDEAS:

1. On a bulletin board or a display area, make large posterboard pictures of a number of different household items. Label the board KITCHEN CHEMISTRY.

2. Display questions to challenge your students' thinking:

   How can you tell an acid from a base?

   What happens when vinegar and baking soda mix?

   What is an emulsion?

   What causes iron to rust?

   How could you stop rust from forming?

EXTRA SPARK STARTER:

1. Perform some science magic:

   There is black carbon in white sugar. Put one cup of sugar in a jelly jar. Pour one-half cup of sulfuric acid over the sugar. Do not let the students get too close — the fumes are strong. Be careful not to get any on your skin — it will burn you. Sulfuric acid can be obtained through a helpful chemistry teacher or a science supply house. The acid drives off all the hydrogen and oxygen in the sugar. A black column of carbon rises out of the jar — very impressive.
   Ask: What is an acid? How can you tell an acid from a base?

2. Have a KITCHEN CHEMISTRY Scavenger Hunt.

Give each student a paper bag with his or her name on it.
Run off the list of materials needed for the KITCHEN CHEMISTRY experiments.
Challenge your students to bring in as many of the items as possible.
Check off the items with each student as they bring in the items.
Arrange an area of shelves to store the items. Put alphabetical cards on the shelves. Let the students help you sort the items into labeled bags and put them on the shelves.
This will be a good experience in sorting and alphabetizing.
This also helps make materials easy to find and easy to put away.

MATERIALS NEEDED:

*Indicator
A work area near a sink
Samples of: ammonia,
  lemon juice, tea,
  laundry soap dissolved in
  water, vinegar, 7-Up,
  baking soda dissolved in
  water, and orange juice
  (Put in labeled baby
  food jars with lids. Make
  several samples of each)
Aluminum foil
Block of wood
Cooking oil
Sandpaper
Pint jars

Plastic straws
Pink and blue
  litmus paper
¼ cup measuring cup
Long-handled spoon
Scissors
Metric ruler
Food coloring
Ball-point pen
Jelly jar
Liquid detergent
Paint brush
½ teaspoon
Iron nails
Rust-resistant
  paint

Plastic cups
Glass pop bottles and
  corks that fit snugly
  in the top
Paper towels (at least
  3 varieties)
Magnifying glass
Clock with a second hand
Turpentine
One-cup measuring cup
Newspapers
White paper
Empty baby food jars
  with lids
Petroleum jelly
Tape

*To prepare indicator, dissolve one laxative tablet containing phenolphathalein in one-fourth cup of rubbing alcohol. Keep this solution stored in a baby food jar with a lid.

If you decide to have a scavenger hunt, you will want to include only items on the list that are needed in quantity.

ADDITIONAL SOURCES: BOOKS

Cobb, Vicki. Science Experiments You Can Eat. Lippincott Co., 1972.

Goldstein-Jackson, Kevin. Experiments With Everyday Objects. Prentice-Hall, Inc., 1978.

Stone, Harris, and Bertram M. Siegel. Puttering With Paper. Prentice-Hall, Inc.

Wyler, Rose. What Happens If . . ? Walker and Co., 1974.

ANSWERS:

Ask students to answer thought questions in complete sentences.

p. 99:	ACID	BASE
	Lemon juice	Ammonia
	Tea	Laundry soap

p. 100:	ACID	BASE
	Vinegar	Baking soda
	7-Up	
	Orange juice	

p. 101: 1. The vinegar and baking soda fizzes and foams. The cork pops out of the bottle. Some students may mention that the mixture seems to expand and that a gas escapes from the bottle.

2. The reaction could be made stronger by using more vinegar and baking soda. Shaking harder can increase the reaction somewhat. A tall, narrow bottle with a small opening would increase the force of the reaction.

p. 102: Answers will vary. In general, the "why" should relate to the number of holes. The more holes the paper has, the more water can rise quickly through it.

p. 104: Chart results will vary. They should be nearly the same in test 1 and 2.

1. It is important to do two tests because if the tests are about the same, then the results can be assumed to happen repeatedly. If the results are very different, no general conclusion can be made. A scientist will repeat the same tests many times.

p. 105: 5. The picture and printing will be reversed on the print.

p. 106: 1. The oil forms a layer on top of the water.
2. In the jar with soap, the oil is in drops.

p. 107: Answers will vary. Check for thoughtful responses.

p. 108: Answers to the questions will vary depending on whether the test that the student chooses to try speeds up rusting or slows it down. Check for logical responses.

p. 109: 1. The nail in the water started to rust first.
2. The nail in the water had more rust.

EVALUATION:

Match each sentence to an answer from the list. Put the letter of the correct answer on the blank.

A. Emulsion   C. Color   E. An acid
B. A base   D. Rust

1. Phenolphathalein turns pink in __(B)__ .

2. An indicator changes __(C)__ to show an acid or a base.

3. Vinegar is __(E)__ .

4. In an __(A)__ tiny drops of one liquid are spread evenly through the other liquid.

5. A combination of iron and oxygen forms __(D)__ .

Number in order the steps to making a kitchen printing press.

__(4)__ Press wood on paper

__(5)__ Peel off white paper

__(3)__ Brush turpentine mixture over the entire picture

__(2)__ Mix turpentine, water, and liquid detergent

__(1)__ Cut out a picture

EXTENDED LEARNING:

1. Try other brands of paper towels to find which one is the champion water absorber.

2. Try other experiments with acids and bases.

3. Try other kinds of kitchen printing. Potato printing can be fun.
   To make a potato print, cut a large potato in half.
   Then either cut out a design or cut out around a design.
   Dip the potato into poster paint and press onto construction paper.

4. Test to see if refrigeration slows down rusting.

Name _____

HOW CAN YOU TELL AN ACID FROM A BASE?

You will need: indicator, two plastic straws, two plastic cups, a work area near a sink, and sample jars of ammonia, lemon juice, tea and laundry soap.

Directions:

1. Pour indicator into one cup and ammonia into the other.

2. Keep one straw to use only with the indicator. Put the end of this straw into the indicator. Put one finger over the top of the straw. Some indicator will stay in the straw until you remove your finger.

3. Drop the indicator into the ammonia without letting the straw touch the liquid.

4. If the ammonia does not change color, it is an acid. If it turns pink, it is a base. Put an <u>X</u> on the chart to show the results.

5. Rinse the cup and straw. Test each of the other samples.

TEST SOLUTION	ACID	BASE
Ammonia		
Lemon juice		
Tea		
Laundry soap		

Name _____

HOW CAN LITMUS PAPER BE USED TO IDENTIFY ACIDS AND BASES?

You will need: pink and blue litmus paper, one plastic cup, a work area near a sink, and sample jars of vinegar, 7-Up, baking soda and orange juice.

Directions:

1. Tear each piece of litmus paper in half. You need only a little for each test.

2. Pour some vinegar into the cup. Touch it with a piece of the pink and a piece of the blue litmus paper.

3. If the pink paper does not change and the blue paper turns pink, it is an acid. If the blue paper does not change and the pink paper turns blue, it is a base.

4. Put an X on the chart to show the results. Rinse the cup and test each of the other samples.

TEST SOLUTION	ACID	BASE
Vinegar		
7-Up		
Baking soda		
Orange juice		

WHAT HAPPENS WHEN VINEGAR AND BAKING SODA MIX?

You will need: a glass pop bottle, vinegar, one-fourth cup measuring cup, baking soda, a long-handled spoon and a cork that fits snugly in the bottle.

Directions:

1. Pour about one-fourth cup of vinegar into the bottom of the pop bottle.

2. Tip the bottle to one side.

3. Use the handle of the spoon to put baking soda into the neck of the bottle. Do not let the baking soda fall into the vinegar.

4. Put the cork in the top of the bottle. Be sure that the cork is not pointed at you or at anyone else. Shake the bottle.

Questions:

1. What happens to the vinegar and baking soda? _____

_____

_____

2. Tell one way that you could make this reaction stronger. _____

_____

_____

Name _____

WHICH PAPER CAN SOAK UP THE MOST WATER?

You will need: three different paper towels, scissors, a metric ruler, another ruler to tape the towel strips to, a magnifying glass, three plastic cups, food coloring, a clock with a second hand, a friend, and a ball-point pen.

Name the three kinds of paper towels.

1. _____

2. _____

3. _____

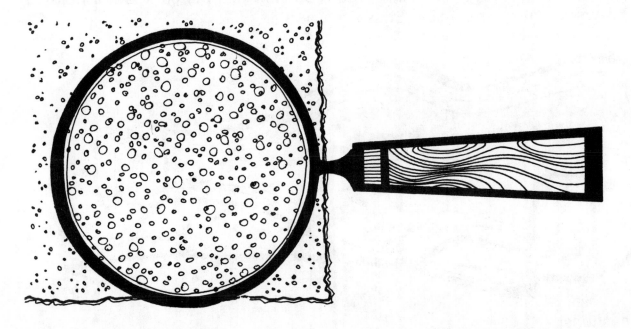

Look at the paper towels with the magnifying glass. Which towel appears to have the most tiny holes? _____

Which towel do you think will be able to absorb the most water?

_____

Why do you think that? _____

_____

_____

Name _____

WHICH PAPER CAN SOAK UP THE MOST WATER — continued

Directions:

1. Cut two strips from each towel. The strips should be twenty centimeters long and eight centimeters wide.

2. Tape one strip of each towel on the ruler. Space them about four centimeters apart.

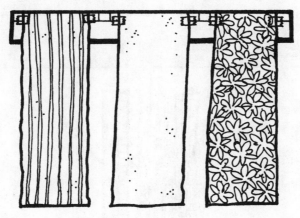

3. Fill each cup half full of water and add two drops of food coloring.

4. Hold the ruler over the cups. Have a friend help you so that the strips touch the water at about the same time.

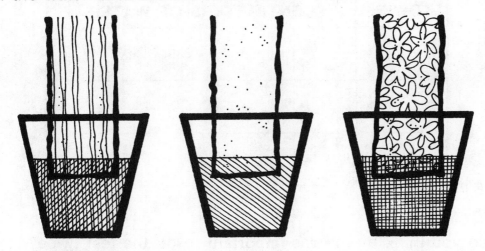

5. Hold the strips in the water for one minute.

6. Take the paper out of the water. Make an ink spot where the wet towel meets the dry towel.

7. Measure how many centimeters of water was soaked up by each towel. Write that number on the chart.

Name _____

WHICH PAPER CAN SOAK UP THE MOST WATER? — continued

TOWEL	CENTIMETERS OF WATER
1	
2	
3	

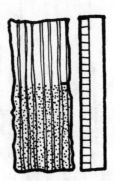

Do the test again with the other strips. Fill in the second chart.

TOWEL	CENTIMETERS OF WATER
1	
2	
3	

Questions:

1. Why do you think that it was important to do the test twice?

_____

_____

2. Which towel absorbed the most water? _____

Name _____

FUN SPOT

You can make your own printing press.

You will need: turpentine, a jelly jar, a measuring cup, liquid detergent, a teaspoon, newspaper, scissors, aluminum foil, a paint brush, white paper, and a block of wood.

Directions:

1. Pour one-half cup of turpentine into the jelly jar. Add one cup of water and two teaspoons of liquid detergent. Stir well. This is your printing liquid.

2. Cut out a newspaper picture with some printing below it. Put the picture on a piece of aluminum foil.

3. Brush the printing liquid over the whole picture. Put a piece of white paper over the wet picture.

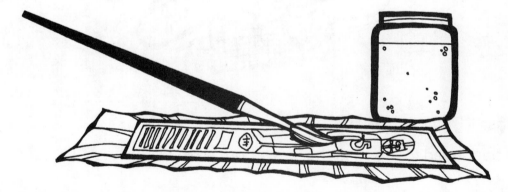

4. Press the paper with the block of wood.

5. Look at your print. How is it different from the newspaper picture?

_____

_____

HOW DOES SOAP WORK?

You will need: two baby food jars with lids, one-half teaspoon, cooking oil, and liquid detergent.

Directions:

1. Fill each jar half full of water.

2. Put one-half teaspoon of cooking oil into each jar.

3. Put one-half teaspoon of liquid detergent in <u>one</u> jar.

4. Put the lids on both jars. Shake the jars well.

Questions:

1. What happened to the oil in the jar without soap? _____

_____

2. In the jar with soap, the oil is

   ☐ in a layer   ☐ in drops

You have just made an *emulsion*. In an emulsion, tiny drops of one liquid are spread evenly through the other liquid.

Name _____

HOW CAN YOU STOP RUST?

Rust is the combination of iron with the oxygen in the air. Rusting can cause metal objects to get holes in them or to crumble away. Here are two ways that you could try to stop rust.

Pick one of these two ways or try an idea of your own. Tell how you will try to stop an iron nail from rusting.

_____

_____

You will need a control. In an experiment, a control is something that is not changed. In your experiment, the control will be an iron nail to which nothing has been done to stop rusting. Be sure that both nails are free of rust before you start. If necessary, rub them clean with sandpaper.

Tell what materials you will need for your experiment:

_____

_____

HOW CAN YOU STOP RUST? — continued

Tell how you will do your experiment. _____

_____

_____

_____

_____

Rust will not appear overnight. Check your test and control nails each day for seven days. Keep the nails in a warm place and sprinkle them with water every other day. Rust will appear as reddish-brown spots.

Questions:

1. How many days did it take for rust to appear? _____

2. Rust first appeared on the

   ☐ test nail.   ☐ control nail.

3. After seven days there was more rust on the

   ☐ test nail.   ☐ control nail.

4. In one sentence, tell what you found out in your experiment. _____

_____

_____

Name _____

DOES WATER SPEED UP RUSTING?

You will need: two iron nails, sandpaper and two pint jars.

Directions:

1. Sand the nails and put one in each jar.

2. Pour enough water in one jar to cover the nail. Add water daily if necessary to keep the nail covered with water.

3. Put the jars side by side in a warm place. This can be inside or outside.

4. Check the nails each day for fourteen days. Rust will appear as reddish-brown spots.

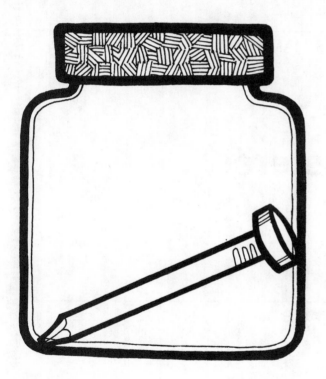

Questions:

1. Which nail started to rust first?

   ☐ The one in the water.   ☐ The one that was dry.

2. At the end of the test, which nail had more rust?

   ☐ The one in the water.   ☐ The one that was dry.

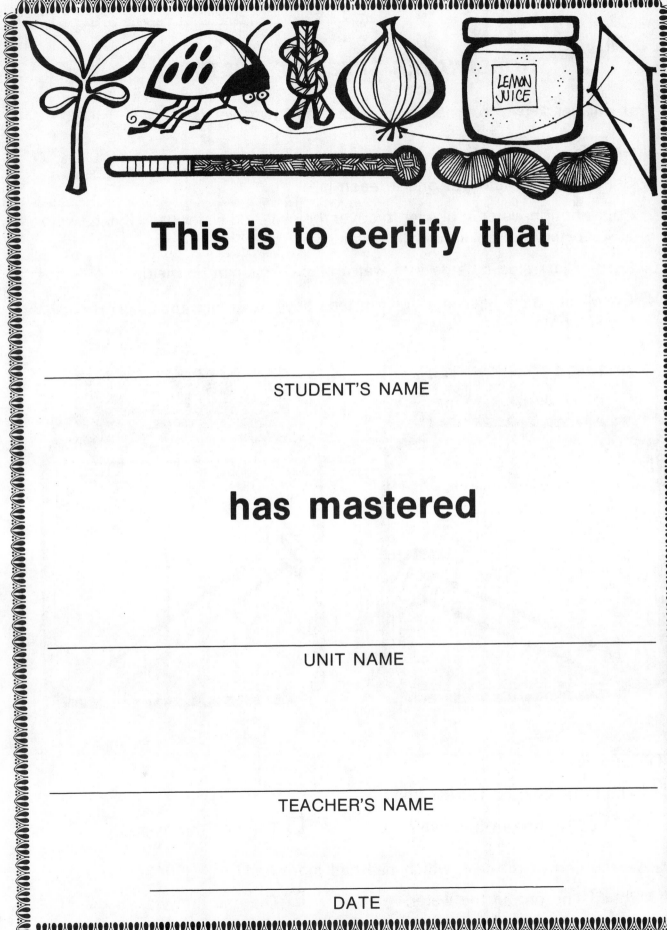

This is to certify that

_____

STUDENT'S NAME

has mastered

_____

UNIT NAME

_____

TEACHER'S NAME

_____

DATE

NOTES

NOTES